Contents Guide

~ Welcome & What You'll Learn

Section 1: Understanding Continuous Integration and Delivery

1. Demystifying CI
2. Embracing CD

Section 2: Setting Up Your DevOps Environment

3. Unveiling the Power of Docker
4. Dockerizing Your Mac Environment
5. Dockerizing Your Windows Environment
6. Dockerizing Your Linux Environment
7. Crafting Your Coding Sanctuary: Editor Selection
8. Launching Jenkins: Your DevOps Command Center
9. Navigating the Portal: A Guide to Logging In

Section 3: Mastering Jenkins Essentials

10. Architecting Your First Job
11. Decoding Jenkins Settings: Part 1
12. Decoding Jenkins Settings: Part 2

Section 4: Navigating Jenkins Pipelines

13. Embarking on the Pipeline Journey
14. Setting Sail with Maven
15. Crafting Your Code Haven: VS Code Configuration
16. Accessing the Jenkins Helm: Login Essentials
17. Scripting the Pipeline: Your DevOps Symphony
18. Triggering Builds: Initiating the DevOps Symphony
19. Your Path to Productivity: Essential Resources
20. Maven Magic: Installing and Configuring Maven
21. Pipeline Prowess: Mastering the Pipeline Statement
22. Agent Allocation: Navigating the Agent Environment
23. Stage Setting: Orchestrating the Stages of Development
24. Tidying Up: The Cleanup Stage
25. Repository Revelations: Cloning Repositories
26. Building Brilliance: Executing the Build Stage
27. Exploring the DIR Command: A Deep Dive
28. Harnessing the Power of DIR: Practical Applications
29. Testing Terrain: Navigating the Test Stage
30. Stage by Stage: Recap and Reinforce

31. Success Signals: Celebrating Build Success and Analyzing Logs
32. Console Chronicles: Understanding Console Output
33. Replay: Revisiting and Refining Pipelines

Section 5: GitHub Integration with Jenkins

34. Setting the Stage: GitHub Integration Essentials, Part 1
35. Preparing Your GitHub Environment: GitHub Integration Essentials, Part 2
36. Polling SCM: Navigating Source Code Management, Part 1
37. Fine-Tuning SCM: Maximizing Source Code Management, Part 2

Section 6: Navigating MultiBranch Pipelines

38. Branching Out: Understanding Branches
39. MultiBranch Pipeline Mastery: Setup Essentials, Part 1
40. MultiBranch Pipeline Mastery: Setup Essentials, Part 2

Section 7: Harnessing the Power of Parameterized Pipelines

41. Parameterized Pipelines Unveiled: An Introduction
42. Putting Theory into Practice: Live Demonstration
43. Boolean Parameters Demystified, Part 1
44. Boolean Parameters Demystified, Part 2
45. String Parameters: Customizing Pipeline Inputs
46. Parameter Tracking: Monitoring Parameter Usage
47. Dropdown Selection Parameters Demystified, Part 1
48. Dropdown Selection Parameters Demystified, Part 2

Section 8: Embracing the World of Variables

49. Variable Exploration: An Introduction
50. Variable Declaration: Defining Your Toolkit
51. Variable Utilization: Harnessing the Power of Variables
52. Navigating Jenkins-Specific Environment Variables, Part 1
53. Navigating Jenkins-Specific Environment Variables, Part 2

Section 9: Mastering Advanced Jenkins Techniques

54. Building a Healthy Pipeline: Understanding Build Health
55. Unraveling Issues: Advanced Troubleshooting Techniques
56. Safeguarding Secrets: Managing Credentials in Jenkins
57. Decoding Jenkinsfile Naming Conventions
58. Juggling Jenkinsfiles: Managing Multiple Jenkinsfiles
59. Putting Theory into Practice: Demystifying Multiple Jenkinsfiles with a Live Demo
60. Debugging Secrets: Advanced Techniques for Troubleshooting
61. Conditional Logic Unleashed, Part 1: Mastering If Statements
62. Conditional Logic Unleashed, Part 2: Advanced If Statements Techniques
63. Function Fundamentals, Part 1: Exploring Functionality in Jenkins

64. Function Fundamentals, Part 2: Advanced Functionality Techniques
65. Scoping Variables: Understanding Variable Scope in Jenkins
66. Bash Brilliance: Executing Multiple Lines in the Bash Shell
67. Job Inception: Creating Jobs from Jobs
68. Passing the Torch: Passing Parameters Between Jobs
69. Expanding Horizons: Exploring Advanced Jenkins Plugins

Section 10: Wrapping Up and Cleaning House

70. Saying Goodbye: Deleting Forked Repositories
71. Closing Shop: Stopping Docker Containers
72. Tidying Up: Deleting Unused Volumes

Section 11: Jenkins Administration

73. System Configuration Essentials: Configuring Jenkins for Optimal Performance
74. User Management: Managing User Accounts and Permissions
75. Plugin Management: Installing, Updating, and Removing Jenkins Plugins
76. Backup and Restore: Safeguarding Your Jenkins Setup
77. Monitoring and Logging: Keeping an Eye on Jenkins Performance
78. Security Best Practices: Securing Your Jenkins Environment

Section 12: Jenkins Integration and Extensibility

79. Integrating Jenkins with Other Tools: Seamless Integration for Enhanced Workflows
80. Extending Jenkins with Custom Plugins: Building and Installing Custom Plugins
81. Integrating Jenkins with Cloud Services: Leveraging Cloud Resources for Scalability
82. Jenkins API: Automating Jenkins Tasks with the REST API
83. Event-Driven Automation: Triggering Jenkins Builds with Webhooks
84. Exploring Jenkins Ecosystem: Discovering Additional Resources and Communities

~ *Conclusion*

Welcome & What You'll Learn

Welcome to the World of DevOps with Jenkins

DevOps. It's one of the most transformative trends in the software industry today. This dynamic approach promises to bridge the gap between development and operations, streamline release cycles, and enhance software quality. But how do you actually make it happen? That's where Jenkins comes in.

Jenkins, the open-source automation server, sits at the heart of a thriving DevOps ecosystem. It provides you with the tools to orchestrate and automate nearly every aspect of your software delivery pipeline. And in this book, "Jenkins: From Beginner to Pro," you'll embark on a journey to master this essential tool.

Why Jenkins?

You might be wondering, why focus solely on Jenkins? Here's why:

- **Open-Source and Extensible:** Jenkins enjoys a massive community ensuring its continued development. With a wealth of plugins, your workflows can be customized to fit your unique requirements.
- **Flexibility:** Jenkins integrates seamlessly with an array of tools and technologies across the DevOps landscape.
- **Ease of Use:** While incredibly powerful, Jenkins boasts a user-friendly interface, lowering the barrier to entry.
- **Automation Powerhouse:** Jenkins will help you automate away repetitive, time-consuming tasks, freeing up your valuable development and operations team efforts.

What You Will Learn

This book is meticulously crafted to guide you through all you need to unlock the full potential of Jenkins in your DevOps endeavors. As you embark on this journey, you'll gain mastery over:

- **DevOps Fundamentals:** We'll begin by building a solid foundation in the principles of Continuous Integration (CI) and Continuous Delivery (CD). You'll learn how Jenkins fits into these transformative methodologies.
- **Jenkins Installation and Setup:** You'll discover how to install and configure Jenkins on various platforms to create your central automation hub.
- **Workflow Creation:** You'll learn to build and manage different types of jobs in Jenkins, automating core development and deployment tasks.

- **Jenkins Pipelines:** You'll unlock the power of Jenkins Pipelines for complex orchestration of build, test, and deployment stages, ensuring seamless and efficient code delivery.
- **GitHub Integration:** We'll deep dive into how to integrate Jenkins with GitHub. This integration empowers you to automatically trigger builds upon code changes, streamlining your workflows.
- **Parameterized Builds:** You'll learn to make your build processes more dynamic and versatile by introducing variables and parameters.
- **Advanced Techniques:** We'll explore advanced topics like build health tracking, secret management, custom plugins, and integration with popular cloud services.
- **Jenkins Administration:** You'll gain the skills to effectively manage and secure your Jenkins environment, guaranteeing optimal performance and reliability.

A Hands-On Journey

This isn't just a theoretical book. Theory is vital, but this book emphasizes hands-on learning. Throughout the chapters, you'll work on numerous practical examples and projects. By getting hands-on, you'll transform concepts into tangible skills and deepen your understanding.

Unlock Your DevOps Potential

Whether you're a developer looking to streamline your processes, an operations engineer eager to reduce manual toil, or a system administrator aiming to automate tasks, this book is designed for you! By the end of this journey, you'll have the skills and confidence to implement robust and scalable DevOps practices that drive your software projects to new heights.

Let's Get Started!

Are you excited to start? Excellent! In the next chapter, we'll establish a foundation by demystifying the fundamentals of Continuous Integration and Continuous Delivery. Buckle up, and let's dive into the exciting world of DevOps with Jenkins!

Important Additional Resources

- **Jenkins Website:** https://www.jenkins.io/
- **Jenkins Documentation:** https://www.jenkins.io/doc/

Section 1:
Understanding Continuous Integration and Delivery

Demystifying CI

The Foundation of Modern Software Delivery

In the fast-paced world of software development, speed and reliability are paramount. Traditional development models often resulted in slow releases, with bugs discovered late in the process, leading to costly fixes and delays. Enter Continuous Integration (CI). This transformative approach has revolutionized the way software is built and released, enabling teams to deliver higher-quality code more frequently.

What is Continuous Integration?

At its core, Continuous Integration is a development practice focused on frequently integrating small code changes into a shared code repository. Each time a developer commits a change, a series of automated processes are triggered:

1. **Build:** The code is compiled and built, ensuring that it functions as a whole.
2. **Automated Testing:** A suite of unit and integration tests are executed, quickly catching any errors introduced by the changes.
3. **Feedback:** Developers receive immediate feedback on the success or failure of their changes. If a build breaks or tests fail, they know exactly where to look to fix the issues.

The Benefits of CI

CI offers a multitude of benefits that optimize the software development process:

- **Catch Bugs Early:** Automated testing uncovers errors quickly. This means that bugs are identified and fixed well before they make their way into production, saving valuable time and resources.

- **Increased Collaboration:** By frequently integrating and sharing code, developers work in tighter sync. This reduces potential merge conflicts and fosters a culture of knowledge sharing.
- **Accelerated Release Cycles:** Since small changes are continuously tested and integrated, software is always in a releasable state. This enables more frequent updates and the ability to deliver new features to users faster.
- **Improved Code Quality:** The continuous feedback loop ensures that every change is tested rigorously. This leads to a more stable and robust codebase.
- **Boosted Developer Confidence:** With every successful build and test passing, developers gain greater confidence in their code changes.

CI Workflow: A Cyclical Journey

Let's visualize a typical CI Workflow to understand how it operates:

1. **Development:** Developers work on their individual feature branches, making changes to the project's source code.
2. **Commit:** Once a developer completes a set of changes, they commit their code to the shared repository.
3. **Build Trigger:** A CI server, like Jenkins, detects the code change and initiates an automated build process.
4. **Compilation:** The code is compiled to verify that it can be transformed into an executable program.
5. **Testing:** A suite of automated tests thoroughly checks the code, including unit tests that validate individual components as well as broader integration tests.
6. **Feedback Loop:** Developers get notified quickly whether the build and tests were successful or if failures occurred, allowing them to address any issues immediately.
7. **Integration:** If the build and tests are successful, the changes are automatically merged into the main code branch.

This cycle repeats itself continuously, ensuring that the project is always in a deployable state, while problems are surfaced before they become major roadblocks.

Jenkins: The CI Maestro

Jenkins plays the role of the orchestrator in this process. It is responsible for:

- Monitoring the shared code repository for changes
- Automating the build process
- Executing test suites
- Providing real-time feedback to developers
- Managing the overall CI process

Looking Ahead

Continuous Integration is an essential cornerstone of modern DevOps practices. Understanding CI gives you the foundation for smoother collaboration and higher quality software. In subsequent chapters, we'll dive into Continuous Delivery, building upon CI to create a complete, automated software deployment pipeline.

Additional Resources

- **What is CI/CD?** (Atlassian):
  https://www.atlassian.com/continuous-delivery/ci-cd
- **Martin Fowler: Continuous Integration**
  https://martinfowler.com/articles/continuousIntegration.html

Embracing CD

Beyond Integration: Automating the Path to Production

In the previous chapter, we explored Continuous Integration (CI). With CI, we established a strong foundation for frequent code changes, automated testing, and rapid feedback loops. Now it's time to take the next step: Continuous Delivery (CD). While CI and CD are often spoken of in tandem, they serve distinct yet intertwined purposes.

What is Continuous Delivery?

Continuous Delivery extends the principles of Continuous Integration to fully automate the software deployment process. The goal of CD is to have your code in a *constantly* deployable state to production, ensuring new features and bug fixes can reach users as quickly and safely as possible.

A true CD pipeline incorporates these key elements:

- **Automated Build and Test:** This forms the backbone, ensuring that every code change passes through rigorous testing.
- **Automated Deployment to Staging:** Once a build passes, it's automatically deployed to a staging environment, a near-replica of production, for further verification.
- **Manual Approval Gates (Optional):** While automation is key in CD, teams may include checks requiring manual approval at critical deployment stages, particularly before production.
- **Automated Production Deployment:** If all prior stages are successful, the changes are automatically pushed into the live production environment.

Contrasting CI and CD

Let's illustrate the distinction:

- **CI:** Focuses on integrating, building, and testing changes in a shared repository. It's about ensuring *code readiness*.
- **CD:** Extends CI to orchestrate the *deployment process* through various environments, all the way to production. It's about ensuring *release readiness*.

The Benefits of CD

Embracing CD brings forth numerous advantages:

- **Lightning-Fast Releases:** CD minimizes the time between a developer committing code and that code going live, enabling faster delivery of value to users.
- **Reduced Risk:** Through automated testing and deployment to staging environments, deployment risk is greatly diminished.
- **Improved Reliability:** The consistency and rigor of a CD pipeline lead to more stable production releases.
- **Enhanced Agility:** Developers can focus on creating great features, confident that the release process is automated and dependable.
- **Empowering User Feedback:** Faster deployment cycles allow for quicker user feedback, enabling teams to rapidly iterate and improve their software.

The CD Pipeline in Action

Let's visualize a typical CD pipeline to understand how it extends a typical CI setup:

1. **CI Cycle:** The CI process we outlined in the previous chapter remains in place, ensuring code changes are built, tested, and merged into the main branch.
2. **Deployment to Staging:** Upon successful integration, the CD process kicks in, automatically deploying the changes to a staging environment.
3. **Staging Tests:** Automated tests designed for staging (e.g., integration tests, performance tests) are executed.
4. **Approval (Optional):** If the workflow dictates a manual approval step, the process pauses and notifies responsible parties to review the changes in staging.
5. **Deployment to Production:** Upon approval (or if no manual approval is required), the changes are automatically deployed to the production environment.

Jenkins: Your CD Orchestrator

Similar to its CI role, Jenkins acts as the conductor of your CD pipeline. It will be responsible for:

- Triggering automated deployments after successful CI builds
- Executing deployment steps across different environments

- Managing manual approval gates
- Providing reporting and visibility into the deployment process

Looking Ahead

In our journey through the DevOps world, we've now established a robust foundation with both CI and CD. The next step is to delve into the nuts and bolts of setting up your DevOps environment. We'll explore the power of Docker for streamlining development and deployment processes.

Additional Resources

- **What is Continuous Delivery?**
  https://www.atlassian.com/continuous-delivery
- **Continuous Delivery vs. Continuous Deployment: What's the Diff?**
  https://www.atlassian.com/continuous-delivery/continuous-deployment

Section 2:
Setting Up Your DevOps Environment

Unveiling the Power of Docker

Why Docker Matters for DevOps

In the realm of software development, achieving consistency across environments is a perpetual challenge. "It works on my machine!" is a phrase that sends shivers down any seasoned developer's spine. Enter Docker, an elegant solution that has transformed how we build, deploy, and manage applications.

What is Docker?

At its heart, Docker is a containerization platform. Think of it this way:

- **Containers:** Lightweight, self-contained packages that include everything your application needs to run: code, libraries, system tools, and dependencies.
- **Docker Engine:** The software that runs on your system, enabling you to build and execute these containers.
- **Docker Images:** Snapshots, or templates, that define the contents and structure of a container.

Docker vs. Virtual Machines

It's important to distinguish Docker from traditional virtual machines (VMs):

- **Virtual Machines:** VMs emulate an entire operating system (OS) on top of your host machine. Each VM requires its own copy of the OS, along with any necessary applications and libraries. This can lead to resource-intensive setups.
- **Docker Containers:** Docker containers share the *kernel* of your host operating system and only bundle application-specific components. This results in a far smaller footprint, increased portability, and lightning-fast startup times.

Key Docker Benefits

Docker offers a multitude of benefits that streamline and optimize your DevOps environment:

- **Environment Consistency:** Docker images ensure that your application runs identically across development machines, testing environments, and production servers. This eliminates the dreaded "works on my machine" syndrome.
- **Portability:** Since Docker containers carry their entire runtime environment, they can be deployed effortlessly across different operating systems and cloud platforms.
- **Simplified Configuration:** All application dependencies are defined within the Docker image, greatly simplifying setup and reducing the potential for misconfiguration.
- **Efficient Resource Utilization:** Docker's lightweight nature allows multiple containers to run on a single machine, making the most of your hardware resources.
- **Microservices Support:** Docker is an excellent fit for microservices architectures, where applications are broken down into smaller, independent services within containers, promoting modularity and scalability.

Docker Workflow

Here's a basic overview of how one works with Docker:

1. **Develop:** You develop your application as usual.
2. **Docker Image Creation:** You write a `Dockerfile`. This serves as a recipe for building your Docker image, specifying all the required dependencies and setup steps.
3. **Build:** You run a Docker command to build the image, resulting in a snapshot.
4. **Run:** You launch a container from your image. The container acts as an isolated environment in which your application executes.

Key Components

Let's introduce some fundamental Docker terminology:

- **Dockerfile:** The text-based blueprint defining the contents and steps for building a Docker image.

- **Docker Images:** The portable package that holds an application, dependencies, and everything needed for it to run. Images serve as the basis for creating containers.
- **Docker Containers:** Isolated, running instances of a Docker image.
- **Docker Registry:** A repository for storing and sharing Docker images. Popular registries include Docker Hub (https://hub.docker.com/), a public registry, and private registries that can be hosted within your organization for secure storage.

Looking Ahead

Now that you have a foundation in Docker, we'll dive into practical examples of how to Dockerize your development environments for various operating systems. By harnessing the power of Docker, you'll soon experience the transformative benefits it offers within your DevOps journey.

Additional Resources

- **Docker Homepage** https://www.docker.com/
- **Getting Started with Docker** https://docs.docker.com/get-started/

Dockerizing Your Mac Environment

Prerequisites

- **macOS:** This guide assumes you have a Mac running a reasonably recent version of macOS.
- **Basic Command-Line:** You should have some familiarity with the Mac terminal and basic commands.

Installing Docker Desktop for Mac

1. **Download:** Begin by downloading Docker Desktop for Mac from the official website: https://www.docker.com/products/docker-desktop
2. **Installation:** Double-click the downloaded .dmg file and follow the standard Mac installation wizard to drag-and-drop the Docker application into your 'Applications' folder.
3. **Launch:** Open Docker Desktop from your 'Applications' folder. You'll see the Docker whale icon appear briefly in your menu bar, signaling that the Docker engine is starting.
4. **Verification:** Open a terminal window and type `docker version`. This should display the installed versions of both the Docker client and server, confirming successful installation.

"Hello, Docker!" A Simple Example

Let's test your Docker setup with a classic first step:

1. **Pull an Image:** To begin, we'll pull (download) an existing Nginx image (a popular web server) from Docker Hub. Run in your terminal:

   ```
   docker pull nginx
   ```

2. **Run a Container:** Now, let's launch a container based on this image:

   ```
   docker run -d -p 8080:80 nginx
   ```

   - Let's unpack this command:
   - `-d`: Runs the container in detached mode (in the background)
   - `-p 8080:80`: Maps port 8080 of your Mac to port 80 inside the container (where Nginx listens)

3. **Verify:** Open your web browser and navigate to http://localhost:8080. You should be greeted by the "Welcome to Nginx!" page.

Docker Commands: A Quick Primer

Here are some essential Docker commands for getting around:

- `docker ps`: Lists running containers
- `docker ps -a`: Lists all containers (including stopped ones)
- `docker images`: Lists downloaded Docker images
- `docker stop <container-id>`: Stops a running container (you can find the container ID from `docker ps`)
- `docker rm <container-id>`: Removes a stopped container
- `docker rmi <image-id>`: Deletes an image

Dockerizing a Development Project

Let's look at a basic example of how you'd dockerize a simple Node.js application.

1. **Project Setup**
    - Create a directory for your project, e.g., `my-node-app`.
    - Inside the directory, create a file named `app.js` with the following content:

    ```
    const http = require('http');

    const server = http.createServer((req, res) => {
        res.writeHead(200, {'Content-Type': 'text/plain'});
        res.end('Hello, Docker!\n');
    });

    server.listen(3000, () => {
        console.log('Server running on port 3000');
    });
    ```

2. **Dockerfile**
    - Create a `Dockerfile` in the same directory:

    ```
    FROM node:alpine
    ```

```
WORKDIR /app
COPY package*.json ./
RUN npm install
COPY . .
EXPOSE 3000
CMD ["node", "app.js"]
```

3. **Build the Image:**

   ```
   docker build -t my-node-app .
   ```

4. **Run a Container**

   ```
   docker run -d -p 3000:3000 my-node-app
   ```

5. **Test:** Open http://localhost:3000 in your browser. You should see "Hello, Docker!"

Looking Ahead

In subsequent chapters, we'll delve into Docker for other operating systems, explore more advanced Docker concepts, and see how Docker integrates perfectly with your Jenkins setup.

Additional Resources

- **Docker for Mac Documentation** https://docs.docker.com/desktop/mac/

Dockerizing Your Windows Environment

Prerequisites

- **Windows 10/11 Pro or Enterprise:** Docker Desktop for Windows requires these specific editions. For Home editions, older Windows versions, or to leverage Linux containers on Windows, you'll need legacy tools like Docker Toolbox (which is a little more involved to set up).
- **WSL 2 Installation:** Docker Desktop uses Windows Subsystem for Linux 2 (WSL 2) as its backend. Follow the instructions here to enable WSL 2 on your system: https://docs.microsoft.com/en-us/windows/wsl/install.

Installing Docker Desktop for Windows

1. **Download:** Get the Docker Desktop for Windows installer from the official Docker website: https://www.docker.com/products/docker-desktop
2. **Installation:** Launch the installer and follow the onscreen instructions. Make sure to select the "Install required Windows components for WSL 2" option during setup.
3. **Start Docker Desktop:** After installation, you can launch Docker Desktop from your Start menu.
4. **Verification:** Open PowerShell or a command prompt (cmd) and run `docker version`. This should display the installed client and server versions, confirming successful installation.

"Hello, Docker!" on Windows

Let's run a simple container to verify your setup:

1. **Pull an Image:** Pull the Nginx image from Docker Hub:

   ```
   docker pull nginx
   ```

2. **Run a Container:** Start an Nginx container:

   ```
   docker run -d -p 8080:80 nginx
   ```

3. **Test:** Open your browser and go to http://localhost:8080. You should see the familiar "Welcome to nginx!" page.

Important Note: File Paths

When using Docker on Windows, there's a key difference in handling file paths:

- **Inside Docker Containers:** Within the container, file paths use Linux-style conventions (`/var/www/html`).
- **Mounting Volumes:** When sharing files between your Windows system and a container, you'll need to translate Windows paths (e.g., `C:\myproject`) to work within the container.

Dockerizing a Development Project (Example)

Let's use a simple Python Flask application to illustrate how you'd dockerize on Windows.

1. **Project Setup**
    - Create a project directory, e.g., `my-flask-app`.
    - Within the directory, create a file named `app.py` containing the following Python code:

      ```python
      from flask import Flask

      app = Flask(__name__)

      @app.route('/')
      def hello():
          return "Hello, Docker from Windows!"

      if __name__ == '__main__':
          app.run(host='0.0.0.0', debug=True)
      ```

    - Add a `requirements.txt` file to your project folder with the content `flask`.

2. **Dockerfile**
    - Create a `Dockerfile` within your project directory:

      ```
      FROM python:alpine

      WORKDIR /app

      COPY requirements.txt ./
      ```

```
RUN pip install -r requirements.txt

COPY . .

EXPOSE 5000

CMD ["python", "app.py"]
```

3. **Build the Image**

```
docker build -t my-flask-app .
```

4. **Run the Container**

```
docker run -d -p 5000:5000 my-flask-app
```

5. **Testing** Open http://localhost:5000 in your browser to see "Hello, Docker from Windows!"

Additional Resources

- **Docker Desktop for Windows** – (https://docs.docker.com/desktop/windows/)
- **WSL 2: A Beginner's Guide** - https://www.howtogeek.com/426749/what-is-wsl-and-how-do-you-use-it/

Dockerizing Your Linux Environment

Prerequisites

- **A Linux Distribution:** This guide assumes you're running a modern Linux distribution (Ubuntu, Debian, Fedora, CentOS, etc.). Most package managers should work seamlessly for installing Docker.
- **Root or sudo Privileges:** Some commands require administrative privileges.

The Advantages of Docker on Linux

Linux, as the birthplace of containerization technologies, enjoys a particularly smooth Docker experience. Advantages include:

- **Native Support:** Docker runs directly on the Linux kernel, resulting in optimal performance and minimal overhead compared to setups involving virtual machines.
- **Mature Tooling:** Docker has been an integral part of the Linux ecosystem for many years, offering powerful and well-integrated tools.
- **Vast Community & Resources:** The wealth of online resources and community support for Docker on Linux is unparalleled.

Installing Docker Engine on Linux

The process varies slightly depending on your Linux distribution. Let's outline the general steps using Ubuntu as an example:

1. **Update and Upgrade:**

   ```
   sudo apt update
   sudo apt upgrade
   ```

2. **Install Dependencies**

   ```
   sudo apt install ca-certificates curl gnupg lsb-release
   ```

3. **Add Docker's GPG Key:**

   ```
   curl -fsSL https://download.docker.com/linux/ubuntu/gpg | sudo
   ```

```
gpg --dearmor -o
/usr/share/keyrings/docker-archive-keyring.gpg
```

4. **Set Up the Repository**

```
echo "deb [arch=amd64
signed-by=/usr/share/keyrings/docker-archive-keyring.g
pg] https://download.docker.com/linux/ubuntu
$(lsb_release -cs) stable" | sudo tee
/etc/apt/sources.list.d/docker.list > /dev/null
```

5. **Install Docker Engine:**

```
sudo apt update
sudo apt install docker-ce docker-ce-cli containerd.io
```

6. **Verify Installation**

```
sudo docker version
```

Note: For other distributions, find specific installation instructions on the official Docker documentation: https://docs.docker.com/engine/install/

Our First Linux Container

Let's welcome ourselves into the world of Docker on Linux:

1. **Pull an Image:**

   ```
   sudo docker pull ubuntu
   ```

2. **Run a Container:**

   ```
   sudo docker run -it ubuntu bash
   ```

   - The `-it` flag provides an interactive terminal session within the container.
3. **Explore:** You're now inside an isolated Ubuntu container! Feel free to issue Linux commands like `ls`, `apt update` (which will only affect the container).
4. **Exit:** Type `exit` to leave the container.

Dockerizing a Development Project (Example)

Let's use a Node.js application to demonstrate a typical development workflow with Docker on Linux.

1. **Project Setup**
    - Create a directory, e.g., my-node-app.
    - Inside, create app.js (content identical to previous chapters' examples).
    - Create requirements.txt with the content flask.
2. **Dockerfile**
    - Create a Dockerfile within your project directory (similar to previous chapters).
3. **Build the Image**

    ```
    sudo docker build -t my-node-app .
    ```

4. **Run the Container**

    ```
    sudo docker run -d -p 3000:3000 my-node-app
    ```

5. **Testing** Access http://localhost:3000 in your browser to see the result.

Additional Resources

- **Docker Documentation** https://docs.docker.com/

Crafting Your Coding Sanctuary: Editor Selection

The Essence of a Powerful Coding Environment

Your code editor or IDE (Integrated Development Environment) is much more than a mere text-editing tool. It's the cockpit from which you orchestrate the entire development experience. A powerful, well-configured editor is essential for a smooth and efficient DevOps workflow. Choosing the right one significantly boosts productivity, enjoyment, and ultimately, the quality of the code you produce.

Factors to Consider When Choosing an Editor

Let's explore some key factors to consider when making this important decision:

1. **Programming Languages & Frameworks:** The core driver in your selection process should be the technologies you primarily work with. Different editors shine with their support and optimizations for specific languages and frameworks.
2. **Features:** Consider what you value most:
    - **Code Completion (Intellisense):** Intelligent suggestions to save you keystrokes.
    - **Syntax Highlighting:** Readable code coloration.
    - **Debugging:** Built-in debugging tools streamline troubleshooting.
    - **Integrated Terminal:** Command-line access within the editor.
    - **Git Integration:** Managing your code's version history effectively.
    - **Search and Refactoring:** Finding things quickly and changing code structure effortlessly.
3. **Performance:** Your editor should feel snappy and responsive, especially with large projects. Speed is a key part of staying "in the zone" while coding.
4. **Customizability:** The ability to tailor the editor with extensions, themes, and keybindings is crucial for personalization, fitting the editor to *your* workflow.
5. **Community and Support:** A vibrant community offers help, plugins, and evidence that the editor will continue to evolve.

Popular Contenders

Here's a breakdown of some popular contenders to give you a starting point:

- **Visual Studio Code (VS Code)**
    - **Pros:** Excellent balance of features, performance, and a massive extension ecosystem. Works exceptionally well on nearly all OSes.
    - **Cons:** Extensive features can feel daunting for beginners at first.
    - **Best for:** A wide range of developers. Suitable for both beginners (who'll grow into its features) and seasoned veterans. A top choice for web development, JavaScript, TypeScript.
- **Sublime Text**
    - **Pros:** Lightning-fast, clean interface. Highly customizable.
    - **Cons:** Not a full-fledged IDE, making feature comparisons tricky.
    - **Best for:** Developers who value sheer speed and tinkering with extensive configurations.
- **Atom**
    - **Pros:** Open-source and hackable. GitHub integration is deeply baked in.
    - **Cons:** Can suffer from performance issues under heavy loads.
    - **Best for:** Developers who want a tweakable editor and those heavily invested in the GitHub ecosystem.
- **JetBrains Suite (IntelliJ IDEA, WebStorm, PyCharm, etc.)**
    - **Pros:** Powerful refactoring, top-notch code completion, and deep understanding of various programming languages.
    - **Cons:** Resource-intensive. Can have a steeper learning curve. Commercial license required for full features.
    - **Best for:** Developers seeking mature IDEs focused on deep language support. Especially strong choices for Java, Kotlin, and related ecosystems.

Beyond the Basics

Let's dive into aspects that take your coding environment to the next level:

- **Extensions and Plugins:** Explore the extension marketplaces for your chosen editor. They unlock incredible possibilities: linters, code formatters, language-specific enhancements, and even themes to make your editor visually appealing.

- **Keyboard Shortcuts:** Mastering keyboard shortcuts for common actions significantly accelerates your workflow. Dedicate time to learning essential shortcuts for your editor.
- **Workspace Settings:** Most editors allow fine-tuning behavior: tab size, line wrapping, code formatting rules, etc. Personalize these settings for optimal comfort and to match your coding style.

The Power of Experimentation

The best way to find your perfect development environment is to try out a few choices. Most popular editors offer free trials or open-source versions. Invest time in each, build a small project, and see how they feel.

Additional Resources

- **VS Code Website:** https://code.visualstudio.com/
- **Sublime Text Website:** https://www.sublimetext.com/
- **Atom Website:** https://atom.io/
- **JetBrains Website:** https://www.jetbrains.com/

Launching Jenkins: Your DevOps Command Center

Prerequisites

- **Java:** Jenkins is built on Java. You'll need either Java Runtime Environment (JRE) or Java Development Kit (JDK) installed (version 8 or newer, but for long-term use, Java 11 is often the sweet spot).
    - Verify Java installation by running `java -version` in your terminal.
- **Method of Deployment:** We'll cover the most common ways to get Jenkins up and running.

Deployment Scenarios

Let's look at the typical scenarios for deploying Jenkins. Choose the one that best suits your needs:

1. **Running Locally:** For initial exploration and experimentation, you can install and run Jenkins directly on your local machine (macOS, Windows, Linux).
2. **Dedicated Server:** For production use, you'll often want a dedicated server (physical machine or a virtual server in the cloud). This allows for scalability, resource control, and a persistent environment.
3. **Containerization with Docker:** Modern DevOps practices often favor packaging Jenkins in a Docker container. We covered Docker in previous chapters; this approach offers portability and isolation.

Method 1: Installing Jenkins Directly

Let's outline how to install Jenkins on major operating systems. **Note:** This is ideal for experimentation. For long-term setups, choose a more robust approach mentioned later.

- **General Steps**
    - **Download:** Get the latest Jenkins installer/package from the official Jenkins website https://www.jenkins.io/download/. You'll choose between a Long-Term Support (LTS) release or a Weekly release. LTS versions prioritize stability, while weekly releases offer the newest features.

- **Installation:** Follow the instructions for your specific operating system. This usually involves a standard installer (for Windows/macOS) or using your operating system's package manager (e.g., `apt-get` on Ubuntu, `brew` on macOS).
    - **Start Jenkins:** The installer usually handles starting Jenkins automatically. If not, you'll find system-specific startup scripts.
- **OS Specific Guides**
    - Follow the detailed instructions on the Jenkins website https://www.jenkins.io/doc/book/installing/.

Method 2: Jenkins on a Dedicated Server

For better control and production readiness, it's recommended to run Jenkins on a dedicated server. Here's a general outline, **noting that the specifics will depend on your chosen infrastructure** (cloud provider, server OS, etc.):

1. **Server Provisioning:** Prepare a server instance (physical or virtual) with your preferred operating system. Ensure it meets Jenkins hardware requirements based on your anticipated scale.
2. **Java Installation:** If not pre-installed, install Java as outlined in the prerequisites section.
3. **Jenkins Installation:** Follow the instructions for your server's operating system regarding Jenkins installation. You might use package managers, download the WAR (Web Application Archive) file, or other methods.
4. **Networking and Security:**
    - Configure firewall rules to allow access to your Jenkins web interface.
    - Consider securing your Jenkins instance with a reverse proxy (nginx, Apache) for HTTPS support.

Method 3: Dockerized Jenkins

If you're comfortable with Docker, this is an excellent way to run Jenkins

1. **Docker Setup:** Ensure you have Docker installed and running based on the earlier chapters on Dockerization.
2. **Pull the Jenkins Image:**

```
docker pull jenkins/jenkins:lts
```

- Choose a different tag (instead of lts) to experiment with recent or specific versions of Jenkins.
3. **Run the Container** (Basic example)

```
docker run -d -p 8080:8080 -p 50000:50000 --name my-jenkins jenkins/jenkins:lts
```

- Adjust network port mappings as needed.

Next Steps: Initial Setup Wizard

1. **Accessing Jenkins:** Upon successful installation, open a web browser and navigate to:
   - `http://localhost:8080` (if running locally)
   - `http://<your-server-ip>:8080` (when on a dedicated server)
2. **Unlocking Jenkins:** Jenkins presents an initial setup wizard. You'll need an admin password printed to the console/logs or to a file on your system.
3. **Plugin Choices:** Choose between 'Install suggested plugins' or 'Select plugins to install'. For beginners, suggested plugins are a good start.
4. **Create Admin User:** Set up your initial administrator account.

Congratulations! You're ready to explore the Jenkins realm!

Additional Resources

- **Jenkins Installation Guide:** https://www.jenkins.io/doc/book/installing/

Navigating the Portal: A Guide to Logging In

Your Jenkins Dashboard: A Mission Control Overview

After successfully deploying Jenkins, your web browser unlocks the gateway to your DevOps automation powerhouse: the Jenkins web portal. Let's break down the key elements you'll typically encounter:

- **Left-Sidebar**
  - **New Item:** The starting point for creating new jobs/tasks
  - **People:** User management (if you have security enabled)
  - **Build History:** Records of past build executions
  - **Manage Jenkins:** The doorway to administrative settings
  - **My Views:** Customizable view to focus on jobs relevant to you
- **Main Central Area:**
  - Listing of your Jenkins jobs/projects
  - Build status summaries (health indicators)
  - System information widgets (if configured)

Understanding Authentication

Jenkins usually protects itself with a security layer. Here's how authentication typically works:

- **Initial Setup:** During the initial setup wizard, you'd have created your first administrator account. You'll use those credentials for your first login.
- **User Management:** For teams, Jenkins allows you to create multiple user accounts. Users might have different levels of permissions (administer, build, view-only, etc.). We'll discuss this in later chapters on administration.

Your First Login

1. **Accessing Jenkins:** Point your web browser to where you installed Jenkins. Typically:
    - `http://localhost:8080` if installed locally on your machine
    - `http://<your-server-ip-address>:8080` if installed on a remote server.

2. **Login Form:** You should see a login screen requesting username and password.
3. **Entering Credentials:** Input the username and password you configured during the initial setup (or that were provided by your Jenkins administrator).
4. **Welcome to Jenkins:** Upon successful login, you'll land on your Jenkins dashboard!

Common Scenarios & Troubleshooting

- **Forgot Password?**
    - If you've forgotten your password and you're the only Jenkins user, this requires resetting the password directly on the server and depends on how Jenkins is installed. Fear not; there are detailed guides in the Jenkins documentation.
- **Security Plugins:** Jenkins may have additional security plugins installed in some environments. These could provide alternative login methods (e.g., LDAP integration, Single Sign-On). Your admin should guide you.
- **Permissions Issues:** If you are part of a team and encounter "Access Denied" errors after logging in, your user account might lack the necessary permissions. Contact your Jenkins administrator for help.

Customizing Your View

As you start creating Jenkins jobs, the main area of the dashboard will populate with these projects. Things to remember:

- **Sorting and Filtering:** Most tables in Jenkins allow you to sort and filter for quick navigation.
- **My Views:** Create personalized views to group and filter jobs that matter most to you.

Beyond the Basics

We've just scratched the surface of the Jenkins UI. Here's what we'll dive into in upcoming chapters:

- **Creating Your First Job:** We'll soon guide you through building your maiden Jenkins project.
- **System Configuration:** We'll take a peek into the administrative settings in 'Manage Jenkins'.

- **Exploring Plugins:** Jenkins plugins enhance functionality. We'll look at finding and installing these powerful extensions.

Additional Resources

- **Jenkins Wiki – Getting Started:**
  https://www.jenkins.io/doc/book/getting-started/
- **Jenkins User Interface Explained:**
  https://www.jenkins.io/doc/book/using/user-interface/

Section 3:
Mastering Jenkins Essentials

Architecting Your First Job

What is a Jenkins Job (or Project)?

In the Jenkins realm, a 'job' (also sometimes called a 'project') represents a set of instructions or a task you want Jenkins to automate. Think of it as a recipe for the specific actions you want Jenkins to orchestrate. Examples of jobs:

- **Build Jobs:** Compile your code, run tests, and package artifacts.
- **Deployment Jobs:** Deploy your newly built software to various environments.
- **Infrastructure Jobs:** Provision servers or cloud resources.
- **Monitoring Jobs:** Run checks and raise alerts if things go wrong.

Types of Jenkins Jobs

Jenkins offers a few core project types. Let's start our journey with the most common one:

- **Freestyle Project:** The ultimate all-rounder. Provides maximum flexibility in configuring the steps of your job, from building to testing to deployment. We'll focus on this type first.
- **Pipeline Project:** Enables you to express your DevOps workflow as code using a Jenkins-specific language within a `Jenkinsfile`. We'll dive into Pipelines in later chapters.

Building Our First Job (Example Scenario)

Let's imagine a simple Java project. Our first Jenkins job will aim to:

1. **Fetch Code:** Pull your project's latest code from a version control system (e.g., GitHub)
2. **Compile:** Compile your Java code.
3. **Run Tests:** Execute a suite of unit tests to ensure quality.

Step-by-Step Creation

1. **A New Beginning:** From the Jenkins dashboard, click on "New Item."
2. **Name:** Enter a meaningful name for your job (e.g., "MyJavaProject-Build").
3. **Choose a Style:** Select "Freestyle project" and click "OK."
4. **Configuration Playground:** You'll be led to the job configuration screen. This is the heart of your job definition. Let's break down the key areas:
   - **Source Code Management:**
     - Select the version control system you use (like "Git"). Configure the details of your repository. (We'll go in-depth about Git integration in future chapters.)
   - **Build Triggers:**
     - Here, you can choose when your build should run. For now, let's keep it simple and stick with "Build manually." We'll explore automated triggers later on.
   - **Build:**
     - Click "Add build step" and choose an appropriate option based on your project. In our Java example, you'd likely choose "Invoke Maven" and then select goals like 'clean' and 'package.'
   - **Post-Build Actions:** This is where you might do things like archive artifacts or send notifications.
5. **Save:** Click "Save" to preserve your job configuration.

Execution: Manual Trigger

1. **Back to the Dashboard:** You'll return to the dashboard. Locate your newly created job.
2. **Build Now:** Click "Build Now" on the left side of your job listing.
3. **Behold - The Build:** A build will be initiated. You can click on the Build number in the 'Build History' to monitor real-time progress and the console output!

Next Steps: Analyzing the Results

Upon completion, you can:

- **Console Output:** Examine the logs to see if every step ran successfully.

- **Artifacts:** Check if build outputs (such as a packaged JAR file in our Java example) were created.
- **Test Reports:** If you had configured your job to run tests, you can usually find a test results report within Jenkins.

Additional Resources

- **Jenkins Documentation (Creating a new job):**
  https://www.jenkins.io/doc/book/using/using-new-job/

Decoding Jenkins Settings: Part 1

Why Settings Matter

Jenkins offers extensive customization options. Mastering its settings is essential for:

- **Tailored Workflows:** Adapt Jenkins to match your unique development processes.
- **Streamlining Automation:** Configure builds to run efficiently and seamlessly.
- **Optimizing Performance:** Fine-tune Jenkins to make the most of your hardware or infrastructure.
- **Security & Compliance:** Enforce security measures important for your project or organization.

Navigating to "Manage Jenkins"

Your key to customization lies in the "Manage Jenkins" section, accessible from your Jenkins dashboard's left-hand sidebar. Let's break down the top-level categories you'll encounter:

1. Configure System

- **Core Jenkins Settings:**
    - Jenkins Location (the URL where it's accessible)
    - System Message (a customizable banner on the Jenkins dashboard)
    - System Admin e-mail address (for notifications)
    - Number of Executors (how many builds Jenkins can run simultaneously)
- **Tools & Actions:**
    - Configure Global Tool installers (Maven, Java, etc.) and their locations. These tools can be used in your build jobs.
- **Security:** We'll dive deeper into users, authorization, and security settings in later chapters.

2. Global Security Configuration

- **Authentication:** Choose your security realm –
    - Jenkins' own user database (basic)
    - LDAP (integration with directory services like Active Directory)

- o Delegate to servlet container (for advanced integrations)
- **Authorization:** Choose your strategy –
  - o Anyone can do anything (beware - not for production!)
  - o Matrix-based security (fine-grained control over who can do what)
  - o Legacy mode (older, less flexible option)
- **Markup Formatter:** How Jenkins should render text in descriptions (Safe HTML, Plain text, etc.)

3. Configure Global Tools

- **Locations of Key Tools:** Here's where you specify the paths or configurations for crucial tools your builds will need:
  - o JDK installations
  - o Ant installations
  - o Maven installations

4. Manage Nodes and Clouds

- **Nodes:** Jenkins can distribute builds to multiple machines (nodes). We will explore nodes and cloud integration as your DevOps workflows become more complex.

5. Manage Plugins

- **The Heart of Jenkins Modularity:** Plugins are the building blocks that extend Jenkins. Manage, install, update and even learn about available plugins here. We'll dedicate a separate chapter to this powerful feature.

6. System Information

- **A Snapshot of Your Setup:** A centralized view of your Jenkins environment's details, installed plugins, and system properties. Useful for troubleshooting.

7. System Log

- **Jenkins' Diary:** Examine logs for diagnostics. You can configure log levels and what gets captured here.

8. Load Statistics

- **Jenkins' Vital Signs:** Keep an eye on your Jenkins instance's health and performance indicators.

9. Script Console

- **Power User Territory:** Run Groovy scripts directly on your Jenkins instance for advanced tasks and on-the-fly modifications. (Use with caution!)

10. Troubleshooting

- **Various Administrative Tools:** Access specialized tools for troubleshooting specific scenarios

Important Considerations

- **Changes take effect:** Often, changes to settings require a restart of Jenkins or reloading the configuration.
- **Documentation is your friend:** Each section usually has a "Help" link offering detailed explanations.

Part 2 Preview

In the next part, we'll delve deeper into security, node management, and explore some essential plugins.

Decoding Jenkins Settings: Part 2

Let's continue our configuration deep-dive! In this chapter, we'll tackle security fundamentals, explore build nodes, and touch upon the powerful world of plugins.

Security Foundations

Let's revisit "Manage Jenkins" -> "Configure Global Security"

- **Authentication Strategy:**
    - **Jenkins' own user database:** Suitable for smaller setups. Manage users directly in Jenkins.
    - **LDAP** Integrate with directory services like Active Directory for centralized user management.
    - **Unix user/group database:** Leverages user accounts from your Linux server.
- **Authorization Strategy**
    - **Matrix-based security:** Fine-grained control. Assign individual permissions (administer, build, view, etc.) to users and groups.
    - **Project-based Matrix Authorization Strategy:** Even finer control by applying the matrix-based approach to a specific job/project.

Security Best Practices

- **Strong Passwords:** Enforce policies within Jenkins or leverage LDAP's password rules.
- **Principle of Least Privilege:** Grant only the necessary permissions to users.
- **Avoid "Anyone can do anything":** This is tempting for testing but disastrous for production!

Managing Nodes

Let's head to "Manage Jenkins" -> "Manage Nodes and Clouds"

- **Nodes: The Workhorses**
    - Jenkins can delegate builds to other machines (physical or virtual). These become "nodes."
    - **Master:** Your main Jenkins instance is the master node by default.

- **'Dumb' Agent:** Executes build steps as instructed by the master. Temporarily added, does what it's told.
- **Permanent Agent:** Long-lived nodes (e.g., dedicated build machine) better for ongoing work.

Node Setup (Example)

1. **New Node:** Click "New Node," give it a name, choose "Permanent Agent."
2. **Launch Method:**
   - **Launch agent by connecting it to the master:** Common for agents behind firewalls. You get instructions to run on the remote agent machine.
   - **Launch agent agents via SSH:** If you have SSH access to the remote machine. Enter the host and login credentials.
3. **Remote Root Directory:** Path on the agent machine where Jenkins works.
4. **Usage:** 'Use this node as much as possible' (common) vs. restricting to specific job types.

Note: Node provisioning often involves installing Java, tools, and setting up communication with the Jenkins Master, which can get a little more intricate for production scenarios.

The Plugin Universe

Navigate to "Manage Jenkins" -> "Manage Plugins". Prepare to be amazed! This is where Jenkins' true adaptability shines.

- **Tabs:**
  1. **Available:** Plugins you can install.
  2. **Installed:** What's already in your Jenkins environment.
  3. **Updates:** Plugins with newer versions available.
- **Workflow:**
  1. **Filter/ Search:** Hunt for a specific plugin (e.g., "GitHub", "Slack").
  2. **Select:** Check the box next to a plugin.
  3. **Install:** Choose "Download now and install after restart" (safest option).
- **Post-Restart:** Jenkins needs to reload for changes to take effect.

Popular Plugins (Just a Taste)

- **GitHub:** Deep integration with GitHub for source code, triggering builds, etc.
- **Blue Ocean:** Sleek, modernized user interface.
- **Pipeline (and the Pipeline family):** Essential for modern CI/CD pipelines.
- **Mailer:** Send email notifications on build results.
- **Docker:** Control Docker containers from Jenkins.

Additional Resources

- **Jenkins Security Page:** https://www.jenkins.io/doc/book/system-administration/security/
- **Jenkins Wiki - Nodes:** https://www.jenkins.io/doc/book/managing/nodes/
- **Jenkins Plugin Index:** https://plugins.jenkins.io/

Section 4:
Navigating Jenkins Pipelines

Embarking on the Pipeline Journey

Let's embark on a journey into the heart of modern Jenkins workflows – Pipelines. We'll uncover their power and lay the foundation for automating your CI/CD processes like a pro.

Why Pipelines Matter

Jenkins freestyle projects are excellent for getting started. But as your DevOps processes become more sophisticated, CI/CD pipelines offer superpowers:

- **Workflow as Code:** Define your entire build, test, and deployment process as a code-like script (usually within a `Jenkinsfile`).
- **Version Control:** Your pipeline script lives alongside your project code, enabling it to evolve, be versioned, and reviewed just like any other code asset.
- **Flexibility:** Model complex processes with stages, parallel steps, and conditional logic.
- **Durability:** Pipelines are designed to be restarted in case of pauses or interruptions.

Introducing the 'Pipeline' project type

1. **New Pipeline:** From your Jenkins dashboard, click "New Item."
2. **Pipeline Project:** Choose "Pipeline" and give your project a name.
3. **Behold - The Pipeline Editor:** You'll be presented with a built-in script editor and a simple initial script.

Pipeline Syntax: The Basics

While we'll have a dedicated chapter on Pipeline syntax, let's get a quick taste:

- **Declarative vs. Scripted:** Jenkins supports two main flavors of Pipeline syntax:
    - **Declarative:** More structured, opinionated, and easier to get started with. We'll begin here.
    - **Scripted:** Based on Groovy—offers more raw power and flexibility for highly customized scenarios.

Anatomy of a Simple Declarative Pipeline

```
pipeline {
    agent any  //Can run on any available agent

    stages {   //Defines the phases of your pipeline
        stage('Build') {
            steps {
                sh 'mvn clean package' // Example step: Build with Maven
            }
        }
        stage('Test') {
            steps {
                junit '**/target/*.xml' // Example step: Run JUnit tests
            }
        }
    }
}
```

Explanation

- `pipeline { ... }`: The overarching container for your pipeline definition.
- `agent any`: Tells Jenkins to execute the pipeline on any available agent.
- `stages { ... }`: Contains a collection of stages.
- `stage('Build') { ... }`: Defines a stage named 'Build'.
- `steps { ... }`: Contains the actions to be performed within a stage.

Executing Your First Pipeline

1. **Save:** Save your pipeline definition within the 'Pipeline' project configuration.

2. **Build Now:** Click "Build Now" to trigger the pipeline.
3. **Monitoring:** Jenkins will visualize your pipeline's progress. You can view logs for each step.

Beyond the Basics

We've just scratched the surface! In upcoming chapters, we'll dive into:

- **Advanced Stages & Parallelism:** Run steps in sequence or concurrently for efficiency.
- **Environment Variables:** Access information about your build environment.
- **Post-Build Actions:** Email notifications, artifact archival, deployment triggering, and more.
- **Jenkins Shared Libraries:** Create reusable pipeline functions.

Additional Resources

- **Jenkins Pipeline Documentation:**
  https://www.jenkins.io/doc/book/pipeline/
- **Declarative Pipeline syntax walkthrough:**
  https://www.jenkins.io/doc/book/pipeline/syntax/

Setting Sail with Maven

Let's integrate Jenkins with Apache Maven, a powerful ally in managing your Java project lifecycle.

What is Maven, and Why Does It Matter?

Maven is a build automation tool and project management system primarily used in the Java world. Think of it as your ship's navigator and shipbuilder in one:

- **Standardized Project Structure:** Maven promotes conventions for how Java projects should be organized (source code placement, dependencies, etc.), bringing order to the development seas.
- **Dependency Management:** Fetches necessary libraries (JAR files) for your project from repositories, simplifying the process.
- **Lifecycle Goals:** Maven defines a clear lifecycle of phases (e.g., 'compile', 'test', 'package', 'deploy'). You tell Maven *what* to do, and it handles the intricate steps.

Benefits for Jenkins

1. **Pipeline Simplification:** Your Jenkins pipelines lean on Maven to perform core build tasks, making your `Jenkinsfile` cleaner.
2. **Reusability:** Maven concepts extend beyond individual Jenkins jobs. Your developers benefit from the same structure locally.
3. **Ecosystem Access:** Vast repositories of libraries (Maven Central) at your fingertips.

Maven Fundamentals

- **POM file (`pom.xml`)** The heart of a Maven project. This file houses:
    - Project metadata (name, group ID, version)
    - Dependencies (list of libraries your project needs)
    - Build plugins (for customizations)
- **Lifecycle Goals** Examples:
    - `clean`: Deletes build artifacts
    - `compile`: Compiles your source code
    - `test`: Runs your unit tests
    - `package`: Creates a deployable package (JAR, WAR)

Installing Maven

Prerequisites: Make sure you have Java (JDK) installed.

1. **Download:** Get the Maven zip file from the official site: https://maven.apache.org/download.cgi
2. **Extract:** Unzip the file to your desired location (e.g., `C:\Program Files\Apache\maven`)
3. **Environment Variables:**
   - Add `M2_HOME` variable pointing to your Maven installation.
   - Update your PATH to include `%M2_HOME%\bin`.
4. **Verification:** Open a terminal and type `mvn -version`. You should see Maven version info.

Integrating Maven with Jenkins

Jenkins usually has Maven pre-configured or allows easy installation:

1. **Global Tool Configuration:** Go to "Manage Jenkins" -> "Global Tool Configuration".
2. **Locate Maven:** You might find a Maven section. If not, you'll likely be able to click 'Add Maven' to install a Maven instance.
3. **Give it a Name:** This name will be used to reference this Maven installation in jobs.

Our Maiden Maven Build (Example)

Let's enhance a Jenkins job from previous chapters to use Maven. Assuming you have a simple Java project:

1. **Adjust your Jenkinsfile:**

```
pipeline {
    agent any

    stages {
        stage('Build') {
            steps {
                sh 'mvn package'    // Replaces manual build steps
            }
        }
```

```
            // Keep your 'Test' stage as before ...
        }
    }
```

2. **POM in the Root:** Make sure your Java project has a pom.xml in its root directory.
3. **Build and Behold:** Run your Jenkins job. Jenkins will use your configured Maven to execute the build!

Additional Resources

- **Maven website for detailed guides:** https://maven.apache.org/
- **Maven in 5 Minutes (Intro)**
  https://maven.apache.org/guides/getting-started/maven-in-five-minutes.html

Crafting Your Code Haven: VS Code Configuration

Let's transform VS Code into the perfect companion for your Jenkins pipelines and general development workflow. This chapter will highlight how to customize VS Code to streamline your CI/CD experience.

Why Customize VS Code?

While VS Code shines out of the box, strategic configuration will:

- **Boost Efficiency:** Speed up pipeline authoring and code editing with tailored settings and extensions.
- **Enhance Jenkins Integration:** Optimize the editor for seamless interaction with your Jenkins server.
- **Supercharge Your Workflow:** Make VS Code an even more potent tool in your broader development process.

Key Areas of Customization

1. **Essential Extensions**
    - **Jenkins Pipeline Support:** Install extensions tailored to working with Jenkins Pipelines. These offer syntax highlighting, validation, and snippets for faster `Jenkinsfile` authoring. Search for "Jenkins" in the VS Code Marketplace (https://marketplace.visualstudio.com/vscode).
    - **Language Support:** Ensure you have extensions for Java (Maven projects), Python, or any languages you primarily use. Add linters and formatters for these languages to help maintain code quality.
2. **Pipeline-Focused Settings**
    - **Tab Size:** Match the indentation used in your pipeline scripts for visual consistency.
    - **Word Wrap:** Consider enabling word wrap for long lines in `Jenkinsfiles`, especially within complex declarative pipelines.
    - **Integrated Terminal:** Configure your preferred shell, so it's ready for pipeline testing and interactions with Jenkins.
3. **Workflow-Enhancing Settings and Extensions**
    - **Themes and Icon Packs:** Choose a theme that suits your eyes and personal style. Icon packs help visually distinguish file types.

- **Git Integration:** VS Code's built-in Git support is fantastic. Add GitLens and similar extensions for even more Git superpowers.
- **Remote Development (SSH, Containers):** If your build environments are remote, these extensions will allow you to edit code directly on them.

Example Configuration Steps (VS Code)

1. **Jenkins Extension:**
   - Open the Extensions Marketplace (`Ctrl+Shift+X`).
   - Search for "Jenkins CI/CD" or "Jenkins Pipeline".
   - Install an extension like "Jenkins Pipeline Language Support".
2. **Java Extension Pack (If relevant):**
   - Search for "Java Extension Pack" for a suite of language support tools.
3. **Settings Tuning:**
   - Go to File -> Preferences -> Settings (`Ctrl+,`)
   - Search for settings like:
     - `editor.tabSize`
     - `editor.wordWrap`
     - `terminal.integrated.shell.*` (to adjust your default shell)

VS Code + Jenkins: A Development Powerhouse

Let's make this practical with a scenario tailored to your tech stack:

Scenario: Java with Maven

- **Required Extensions:**
  - Jenkins Pipeline Language Support
  - Java Extension Pack
  - Maven for Java
- **Recommended Extensions:**
  - Spring Boot Tools (if using Spring framework)
  - XML (for editing your Maven `pom.xml`)
  - Test Runner for Java (for running unit tests)
- **Key Settings:**
  - `java.home`: Point to your JDK installation
  - `maven.terminal.useJavaHome`: To ensure Maven uses the correct Java version within VS Code

Additional Resources

- **VS Code Documentation** https://code.visualstudio.com/docs
- **Popular VS Code Extensions for Developers**
  https://github.com/viatsko/awesome-vscode

Pro Tip: Explore keyboard shortcuts in VS Code for frequently used tasks related to Pipelines and Git.

Accessing the Jenkins Helm: Login Essentials

Let's dive into the world of Jenkins Helm charts and outline how to manage user authentication, ensuring secure access to your Jenkins installation.

Why Helm?

Helm, the Kubernetes package manager, offers a streamlined way to deploy and manage Jenkins within a Kubernetes environment. Understanding login mechanisms when using a Helm deployment of Jenkins is crucial for controlling access to your CI/CD control center.

Prerequisites

- **Kubernetes Cluster:** You should have a running Kubernetes cluster. If this is new, consider using a managed service like AWS EKS, Azure AKS, or Google Kubernetes Engine.
- **Helm:** Make sure Helm is installed on your system.
- **Jenkins Helm Chart:** We'll assume you've used Helm to deploy Jenkins. If not, the official Jenkins chart documentation is a valuable resource.

Authentication Strategies with Jenkins Helm

The Jenkins Helm chart supports a few authentication methods. Your organization's security needs will drive the best choice:

1. **Default: Jenkins' Own User Database**
    - Simplest to get started with.
    - Users are managed directly inside Jenkins.
    - Suitable for smaller deployments or testing.
2. **Delegated Authentication: LDAP, OAuth, etc.**
    - Integrates with an existing directory service (Active Directory, etc.) or identity provider.
    - Centralizes user management, improving security in larger installations.

Scenario: Starting with Default Authentication

Let's focus on the initial access with the default user database. The official Jenkins Helm chart documentation will have the most up-to-date details if you've deployed Jenkins using Helm. Usually, you'll do the following:

1. **Retrieve Admin Password:**

- Use `kubectl` to get the name of your Jenkins pod.
- Run the following (replacing `your-jenkins-pod-name`):

```
kubectl exec -it your-jenkins-pod-name cat /var/jenkins_home/secrets/initialAdminPassword
```

2. **Access Jenkins:**
   - Use port-forwarding if necessary to access the Jenkins web interface from your machine.
3. **Login:** Use username 'admin' and the retrieved password.
4. **Follow the Setup Wizard:** Jenkins will guide you through initial setup. Create additional users as needed.

Next Steps: Exploring Authentication Options

1. **Security First:** If your Jenkins will be used seriously, invest time in integrating with a robust authentication system (like LDAP) if your environment supports it. This is essential for security and manageability.
2. **Helm Configuration:** The Jenkins Helm chart offers customization points for:
   - Enabling different authentication modes
   - Configuring LDAP parameters
   - Specifying OAuth settings

Important Considerations:

- **Helm Release vs. In-Jenkins Changes:** Some authentication settings are configured in your Helm values file, impacting the deployed instance. Others are changed post-installation within Jenkins itself.
- **RBAC (Role-Based Access Control):** Combine authentication with Jenkins' authorization mechanisms. You'll need a strategy for assigning roles and permissions for fine-grained access control.

Additional Resources

- **Jenkins Helm Chart Repository:** (https://github.com/jenkinsci/helm-charts)
- **Kubernetes RBAC Documentation:** (https://kubernetes.io/docs/reference/access-authn-authz/rbac/)

Scripting the Pipeline: Your DevOps Symphony

Let's dive headfirst into the expressive power of Jenkins pipeline scripts and how they orchestrate your DevOps workflows.

The Essence of a Jenkins Pipeline as Code

At its heart, a Jenkins pipeline is a codified definition of the steps required to build, test, package, and deploy your software. By using a script, you gain:

- **Automation:** Your CI/CD process becomes consistent and repeatable.
- **Version Control:** Track changes to your build process like other code, enabling rollbacks and collaboration.
- **Flexibility:** Model complex workflows with stages and logic.
- **Reusability:** Pipelines become reusable modules within your DevOps toolkit.

Types of Pipeline Syntax

Jenkins supports two primary flavors:

1. **Declarative Pipelines**
   - Opinionated and structured, designed to promote readability and best practices.
   - A good starting point, especially for simpler pipelines.
   - Example structure:

     ```
     pipeline {
         agent any
         stages {
             stage('Build') { ... }
             stage('Test') { ... }
         }
     }
     ```

2. **Scripted Pipelines**
   - Based on the Groovy programming language.
   - Offers maximum power and flexibility for complex or highly tailored scenarios.
   - Example structure:

     ```
     node {
         stage('Build') { ... }
         stage('Test') { ... }
     ```

}

Mastering the Fundamentals

Whether you focus on Declarative or Scripted, core elements include:

- **node:** Represents an agent (a machine) where work gets executed.
- **stage:** A logical grouping of steps, visualizing progress in the Jenkins UI.
- **steps:** Individual tasks like:
    - `sh`: Execute shell commands (e.g., `sh 'gradle build'`)
    - `git`: Clone a Git repository
    - `junit`: Run JUnit tests
    - `archiveArtifacts`: Store build outputs
    - `mail`: Send email notifications

Declarative Example: A Mini-Pipeline

```
pipeline {
    agent any

    stages {
        stage('Build') {
            steps {
                sh 'mvn package'
            }
        }
        stage('Test') {
            steps {
                junit '**/target/*.xml'
            }
        }
        stage('Deploy to Dev') {
            steps {
                sh 'scp -r target/myapp.jar user@devserver:/path/to/deploy'
            }
        }
    }
}
```

Leveling Up: Moving Towards Scripted

While initially Declarative syntax is easier, Scripted Pipelines unlock more potential:

- **Variables:** For dynamic values within your pipeline.
- **Conditional Logic:** `if/else` statements for decision-making.
- **Looping:** For repeated actions based on conditions or iterating over data.

Additional Resources

- **Jenkins Declarative Pipeline Docs:**
  https://www.jenkins.io/doc/book/pipeline/syntax/
- **Jenkins Scripted Pipeline Docs:**
  https://www.jenkins.io/doc/book/pipeline/syntax/

Practical Tips

- **Start Simple, Then Evolve:** Begin with a basic Declarative pipeline, then incrementally add elements and refactor into Scripted where needed.
- **Version Control Everything:** Store your `Jenkinsfile` in your project's repository.
- **Leverage the Snippet Generator:** Jenkins has a built-in tool to help write pipeline steps (Manage Jenkins -> Configure System -> Pipeline: Snippet Generator)
- **Test-Driven Pipelines:** Consider ways to test your pipeline scripts themselves to prevent introducing errors.

Triggering Builds: Initiating the DevOps Symphony

Let's explore the diverse ways to start your Jenkins pipelines, setting your DevOps processes into motion!

Why Build Triggers Matter

How your Jenkins pipelines get kicked off is a crucial aspect of automating your CI/CD workflow. The right triggering strategy ensures:

- **Responsiveness:** Changes to your code quickly translate into builds to get rapid feedback.
- **Efficiency:** Builds aren't triggered unnecessarily, wasting resources.
- **Adaptability:** Your processes adjust to different development models or scenarios.

Types of Build Triggers

Jenkins offers a variety of mechanisms to start your pipelines:

1. **Manual**
    - The classic 'Build Now' button in the Jenkins interface.
    - Useful for on-demand execution, testing, or troubleshooting.
2. **Scheduled (Poll SCM)**
    - Periodic checks against your source control system (like Git) for any changes.
    - Syntax Example (cron-like): H */4 * * * (Run every four hours)
    - Suitable for scenarios where regular builds are needed.
3. **Webhook Triggers (e.g., GitHub)**
    - Jenkins receives an HTTP payload from your source control system when events occur (push, pull request).
    - Excellent for true, event-driven CI/CD to react immediately to code changes.
4. **Upstream Builds**
    - Pipelines triggering other pipelines.
    - Promotes chaining and dependencies in your DevOps workflows ("Job Inception!")
5. **Remote Triggers (Jenkins API)**
    - External systems use the REST API to start builds.

- Enables integration with issue trackers, monitoring tools, and more.

Considerations for Choosing Triggers

- **Level of Automation:** Do you want highly automated processes (webhooks) or more control (manual/scheduled)?
- **Source Control System:** Some triggers like webhooks depend on the features of your version control provider.
- **Build Frequency:** How often should your pipeline reasonably run? Avoid overly frequent polling if it's unnecessary.
- **Workflow Dependencies:** Factor in how pipelines might relate to each other.

Deep Dive: GitHub + Webhooks

Let's focus on the popular webhook approach using GitHub as a source control example:

1. **Setup Webhook in GitHub:**
   - Navigate to your repository's settings -> Webhooks.
   - Add a webhook, providing your Jenkins URL and a trigger (e.g., 'push' events).
2. **Configure the Jenkins Pipeline:**
   - **Enable Webhook Triggers:** If using a freestyle project, this may be project-specific; for Pipelines, ensure the necessary plugin is installed ('GitHub' plugin).
   - **Extract Information (Scripted):** If needed, you can write Groovy script to parse data sent by the webhook for advanced use cases.

Additional Considerations

- **Security:** Webhooks can be secured with tokens to ensure only authorized systems trigger builds.
- **Quiet Periods:** Jenkins has a 'Quiet Period' setting to prevent builds from immediately starting in batches if commits are made too close together.
- **Build Parameters:** Some triggers can pass information to the build, making pipelines customizable (more on this in the Parameterized Pipelines chapters).

Additional Resources

- **Jenkins Wiki - Build Triggers:**
  https://wiki.jenkins.io/display/JENKINS/Building+a+software+project#Buildingasoftwareproject-BuildTriggers
- **GitHub Webhooks Documentation**:
  https://docs.github.com/en/developers/webhooks-and-events/webhooks

Your Path to Productivity: Essential Resources

The Quest for Continuous Improvement

Jenkins offers incredible depth, and a spirit of continuous learning will take you far. These resources will be your companions as you deepen your knowledge and optimize your pipelines.

Official Jenkins Documentation

Your first and often most authoritative port of call:

- **Jenkins Handbook** (https://www.jenkins.io/doc/book/) : The comprehensive guide covering core concepts to advanced usage.
- **Pipeline Specific Documentation** (https://www.jenkins.io/doc/book/pipeline/): Deep dive into Declarative and Scripted Pipelines, steps, syntax, and more.
- **Wiki** https://wiki.jenkins.io/: A treasure trove of community-contributed tutorials, examples, and solutions.

Community Hubs

- **Jenkins Subreddit** (https://www.reddit.com/r/jenkinsci/): A vibrant forum. Get help, follow trends, and share knowledge.
- **Stack Overflow (Jenkins Tag)** (https://stackoverflow.com/questions/tagged/jenkins): Search existing Q&A or ask specific questions. Chances are, someone has faced a similar challenge!
- **Jenkins Blog:** (https://www.jenkins.io/blog/) News, releases, and insights from the Jenkins project.

Plugin Pages

Jenkins' extensibility is a superpower. When exploring plugins, always refer to their official pages within the plugin index for accurate documentation and usage examples:

- **Manage Jenkins -> Manage Plugins -> Available Tab**

Domain-Specific Resources

- **GitHub Integration Guide**https://www.jenkins.io/doc/book/using/using-github/: Maximize the Jenkins-GitHub dance.
- **Maven Integration**: Maven's site often has useful tips about its interactions with Jenkins.
- **Language + Framework Communities:** Communities surrounding your languages/frameworks (Java, Python, Node.js, etc.) often have best practices and guides for CI/CD pipelines with Jenkins.

Tips for Effective Resource Use

- **Be Specific with Search Terms:** Include keywords about the technology ("Jenkins Maven"), the issue faced, and any error messages.
- **Date Filters:** For online resources, sometimes use date filters to find more recent solutions, as Jenkins and plugins evolve.
- **Don't be afraid to ask:** If you get stuck, the communities mentioned are usually friendly and supportive.

Continuous Learning in Practice

How can we turn resources into workflow improvements? Let's pick one common optimization area:

Build Performance:

1. **Problem Statement:** Your builds feel slow.
2. **Resource Hunting:**
   - Jenkins Docs: Search for "pipeline performance optimization"
   - Jenkins Wiki: Check for "speeding up Jenkins"
   - Stack Overflow: Search "jenkins slow build" along with relevant technologies you use.
3. **Implementation:** Discover tips (e.g., parallelizing tests, optimizing Maven settings, checking agent resource usage). Apply one change at a time to your pipeline.
4. **Measure:** Did build times meaningfully improve? If not, continue to iterate using newfound knowledge.

Additional Resources

- **CloudBees Website (Creators of Jenkins Enterprise)** (https://www.cloudbees.com/): Whitepapers, webinars, and customer case studies for large-scale Jenkins insights
- **Awesome Jenkins** (Community-curated list): https://github.com/jenkinsci/awesome-jenkins

Pro Tip: Bookmark Your Favorites

Create a browser bookmark folder dedicated to your most-used Jenkins resources. As you solve a tricky problem, add the page that helped!

Let's Choose a Challenge

What's ONE area where you want to enhance your Jenkins Pipelines—finding better error messages, integrating a tool, speeding things up?

Maven Magic: Installing and Configuring Maven

Since Maven often goes hand-in-hand with Jenkins, let's unlock its secrets to streamline your Java development processes.

Maven: The Build Master

At its core, Maven is a powerful project management tool primarily for Java. It orchestrates your build lifecycle:

- **Compilation:** Transforms your Java code into executable form
- **Dependency Management:** Fetches libraries (JARs) your project needs
- **Testing:** Executes your unit and integration tests
- **Packaging:** Bundles your code into deployable units (JAR, WAR, etc.)

Why Maven Matters for Jenkins Pipelines

1. **Standardization:** Maven brings structure to your project, making it easier to define build steps within your Jenkins `Jenkinsfile`.
2. **"Don't Repeat Yourself":** Maven handles common build tasks, letting your pipelines focus on the core logic of your CI/CD.
3. **Vast Ecosystem:** The Maven Central Repository gives you access to a massive collection of libraries.

Installation

Prerequisites:

- **Java Development Kit (JDK):** Make sure you have the JDK installed, not just the JRE. You can type `javac -version` in your terminal to check.

Steps

1. **Download:** Grab the latest binary zip file from the Apache Maven website: https://maven.apache.org/download.cgi
2. **Extract:** Unzip the file to a location of your choice (e.g., `C:\Program Files\Apache\maven` on Windows, `/opt/apache-maven` on Linux/macOS)

3. **Environment Variables:**
   - **M2_HOME:** Set this to point to your Maven installation directory.
   - **Path Update:** Append the Maven bin directory to your PATH (e.g., add %M2_HOME%\bin on Windows).
4. **Verify:** Open a new terminal and type mvn -version. You should see Maven version information.

The Heart of Maven: The pom.xml File

Each Maven project has a pom.xml (Project Object Model) file at its root. Key sections include:

- **Project Coordinates:**
    - groupId: A unique identifier for your organization or project group.
    - artifactId: The name of your specific project.
    - version: Tracks your project's releases (e.g. 1.0.0-SNAPSHOT)
- **Dependencies:** A list of libraries (JARs) your project needs, specified with their own coordinates.
- **Build Plugins:** Plugins to add custom behaviors
    - compiler-plugin (for Java compilation)
    - surefire-plugin (for running tests)
    - And many more!

Configuration Deep-Dive: settings.xml

Maven has two key configuration files:

1. **Global Settings:** Often found in [Your User Home]/.m2/settings.xml - affects all Maven projects for a user.
2. **Project-Specific Settings:** settings.xml in a project's directory – overrides global settings.

Use Cases

- **Custom Maven Repositories:** If you host libraries internally, you configure these here.
- **Proxy Settings:** Necessary if you're behind a corporate proxy server.
- **Mirror Settings:** Optimize downloading by redirecting Maven to a closer mirror.

Maven in a Jenkins Pipeline

Usually, Jenkins has Maven pre-configured or allows easy installation as a tool. Here's a simple pipeline snippet demonstrating Maven goals:

```
pipeline {
    agent any

    stages {
        stage('Build') {
            steps {
                sh 'mvn clean package'
            }
        }
        // Add a 'Test' stage here...
    }
}
```

Additional Resources

- **Apache Maven Getting Started Guide**
  https://maven.apache.org/guides/getting-started/]
- **Maven in 5 Minutes**
  https://maven.apache.org/guides/getting-started/maven-in-five-minutes.html]

Pipeline Prowess: Mastering the Pipeline Statement

Let's dissect the individual building blocks of Jenkins pipelines, giving you the power to craft them with precision and control.

The Essence of a 'step'

At the heart of both Declarative and Scripted pipelines lies the fundamental unit of work: the `step`. A step represents a single task or action your pipeline executes. Jenkins provides an extensive vocabulary of built-in steps, and plugins can add even more! Let's look at common categories:

- **Build Steps:**
  - `sh`: Execute shell commands (`sh 'mvn test'`) or (`bat 'mvn test'` on Windows).
  - `gradle`: Run Gradle tasks (if you use Gradle for your builds).
  - `ant`: Invoke Ant targets (for legacy build systems).
- **Test Steps:**
  - `junit`: Execute JUnit tests, collect results.
  - `robot`: Run Robot Framework test cases (popular for acceptance testing).
- **Deployment Steps:**
  - `scp`: Copy files to a remote server via SCP.
  - `aws-cli`: Interact with Amazon Web Services if you deploy there.
- **Artifact Management**
  - `archiveArtifacts`: Store build outputs for later use or promotion.
- **Notifications:**
  - `mail`: Send email notifications upon build status changes.
  - `slackSend`: Send messages to a Slack channel (requires the Slack plugin).

Declarative Pipeline Example

```
pipeline {
    agent any
```

```
    stages {
        stage('Test') {
            steps {
                junit '**/target/*.xml'
            }
        }
        stage('Package') {
            steps {
                sh 'mvn package'
                archiveArtifacts 'target/*.jar'
            }
        }
    }
}
```

Scripted Pipeline Example

```
node {
    stage('Test') {
        junit '**/target/*.xml'
    }
    stage('Package') {
        sh 'mvn package'
        archiveArtifacts 'target/*.jar'
    }
}
```

Controlling Flow (Scripted)

Scripted pipelines allow you to inject Groovy code for more nuanced control:

```
node {
    try {
        stage('Deploy') {
            sh 'scp app.jar user@prodserver:/path/to/deploy'
        }
        currentBuild.result = 'SUCCESS'
    } catch (Exception e) {
        currentBuild.result = 'FAILURE'
```

```
            mail subject: "Deployment Failed", body: "Check
Jenkins: ${env.BUILD_URL}"
        }
}
```

Key Resources

- **Jenkins Pipeline Steps Reference:** This is your ultimate cheat sheet: (https://www.jenkins.io/doc/pipeline/steps/). Search and explore! Often docs for individual steps are found within a plugin's page.
- **Pipeline Syntax Snippet Generator:** Built into Jenkins for quick assistance (Manage Jenkins -> Configure System -> Pipeline: Snippet Generator)

Advanced Mastery

- **Step Parameters:** Many steps take parameters to modify their behavior (e.g., the `junit` step can take different arguments to select which tests to run).
- **Global Libraries:** If you frequently use custom Groovy scripts within pipelines, consider defining them as shared libraries for reuse and maintainability.
- **"Post" Sections:** Add `post` sections to stages to define actions that run regardless of success or failure (e.g., cleanup or always send notifications).

Pro Tips

- **Be Mindful of Agent Location:** Ensure the step you're using is intended to run on the type of agent you've configured for the pipeline or stage.
- **Credentials:** Some steps might need credentials stored within Jenkins to interact with external systems.
- **Experiment in a Sandbox:** Create test pipelines to play with new steps before introducing them into critical pipelines.

Agent Allocation: Navigating the Agent Environment

Let's embark on a journey into the realm of Jenkins agents, understanding how they form the workhorses of your CI/CD process.

What are Jenkins Agents?

- **Distributed Workforce:** Agents are machines (physical or virtual) where Jenkins pipelines actually execute their steps.
- **Master's Command:** The Jenkins 'Master' node orchestrates and assigns work to available agents.
- **Types of Agents:**
    - **Permanent:** Long-lived nodes, part of your managed infrastructure
    - **Ephemeral/Transient:** Spun up on-demand, often in cloud environments.

Why Agent Allocation Matters

1. **Scalability:** Handle increasing build workloads by adding more agents.
2. **Specialization:** Agents can have different tools, operating systems, or hardware for specific build needs.
3. **Isolation:** Keep build environments separate (e.g., dev vs. production testing).
4. **Security:** Sensitive workloads might run on agents restricted to a secure network segment.

Agent Types In-Depth

- **Master Node as Agent:** In smaller setups, the Jenkins master itself can execute builds (but this is generally not ideal for production, see why in 'Considerations' below).
- **Dumb Agents (SSH):** Jenkins connects to these via SSH, giving you full control over their setup.
- **Docker Agents:** Each build runs within its isolated Docker container, maximizing resource usage and reproducibility.
- **Kubernetes Agents:** Pods on a Kubernetes cluster provide dynamic, scalable agents.

Connecting Agents to the Jenkins Master

The specific process depends on the agent type:

- **SSH Agents:** You'll provide Jenkins with SSH credentials to connect to the remote machine.
- **Windows Agents via JNLP:** Windows machines often connect using Java Network Launch Protocol.
- **Docker/Kubernetes:** Configuration is more involved, with Jenkins needing appropriate access within the container environment.

Key Concepts

- **Labels:** Tags applied to agents to classify their capabilities (`linux`, `maven`, `windows-2019`, etc.). Pipelines can request agents based on labels.
- **Executors:** A 'slot' on an agent where a build can run concurrently. Agents can have multiple executors.
- **Node/Workload Balance:** Monitor how many builds are running on each agent to optimize resource usage.

Declarative Pipeline Example

```
pipeline {
    agent {
        label 'docker && java-11'
    }

    stages {
        // ... your build stages here
    }
}
```

Scripted Pipeline Example

```
node('linux && docker') {
    // ... your build steps on a suitable Docker agent
}
```

Considerations

- **Master as Agent Overload:** Using the Jenkins master itself for builds can lead to performance issues on the Jenkins UI and overall stability if builds are too heavy.
- **Security:** Pay close attention to security, especially how agents connect to the master, to prevent unauthorized access.

Additional Resources

- **Jenkins Wiki - Distributed Builds:**
  https://wiki.jenkins.io/display/JENKINS/Distributed+builds
- **Jenkins Documentation - Managing Nodes:**
  https://www.jenkins.io/doc/book/managing/nodes/

Stage Setting: Orchestrating the Stages of Development

Let's dive into the art of breaking down your CI/CD process into well-defined stages within Jenkins pipelines. This chapter is about structuring your workflow for clarity and control.

Why Stages Exist

- **Logical Grouping:** Stages bundle related steps together, making your pipeline more understandable (e.g., "Build", "Test", "Deploy").
- **Visualization:** The Jenkins UI represents each stage visually, offering a progress overview.
- **Granular Control:** Configure actions to happen when a stage starts, succeeds, or fails.
- **Parallelism:** Potential to run stages in parallel for efficiency in some scenarios.

The Essence of the 'stages' Section

Both Declarative and Scripted pipelines utilize a `stages` section to contain their core work. Here's a simple example:

Declarative

```
pipeline {
    agent any
    stages {
        stage('Build') {
            steps {
                sh 'mvn package'
            }
        }
        stage('Unit Tests') {
            steps {
                junit '**/target/*.xml'
            }
        }
        stage('Deploy to Dev') {
            steps {
                sh 'scp app.jar user@dev-server:/path'
```

```
            }
         }
      }
}
```

Typical Stages

While the specifics are project-dependent, common patterns include:

- **Build:** Compiling your code, producing artifacts.
- **Test:** Unit tests, integration tests, linting (code quality).
- **Package:** Creating deployable units (JAR, WAR, Docker images, etc.).
- **Deploy:** Sending your built application to various environments (Dev, Staging, Production).

Controlling Flow with Scripted Pipelines

Scripted pipelines allow you to inject Groovy logic for more complex stage transitions or behaviors. Here's an example with a manual approval stage:

```
node {
    stage('Deploy to Staging') {
        input 'Deploy to Production?'
        // Deployment Logic Here...
    }
}
```

Beyond the Basics

- **'when' Directive (Declarative):** Introduce conditional logic to decide whether a stage should execute (e.g., only deploy if the branch is 'main').
- **'parallel' (Declarative):** Define a set of stages to run concurrently if independent.
- **'post' Sections:** Actions within a stage that always run for cleanup or notifications (e.g., `post { failure { slackSend color: 'danger', message: "Stage Failed!"} })`

Additional Considerations

1. **Granularity:** How fine-grained do you want your stages to be? Balance visibility with the overhead of managing too many.
2. **Environment Mapping:** As you progress through stages, you likely target different environments. Your pipelines might need to adjust parameters based on the stage.
3. **Promotions:** Think about how a build artifact might get "promoted" through stages upon success.

Resources

- **Jenkins Pipeline Documentation - Stages:**
  https://www.jenkins.io/doc/book/pipeline/syntax/#stage

Tidying Up: The Cleanup Stage

Let's delve into the art of responsible pipeline hygiene, ensuring your Jenkins environment stays efficient and organized.

Why Cleaning Matters

1. **Disk Space:** Builds produce artifacts, logs, and temporary data. Unchecked, this consumes valuable storage.
2. **Clarity:** Old build records can clutter the Jenkins UI, making it harder to find relevant information.
3. **Performance:** Excessively long build histories *may* impact Jenkins performance in some scenarios.
4. **Compliance:** You might have requirements to retain build data only for a specific duration.

Cleanup Strategies within Pipelines

Let's focus on techniques you can employ directly in your Jenkins pipelines, both Declarative and Scripted.

- **deleteDir()** A built-in step to clean up the workspace at the end of a build (or at specific points within your pipeline). Example: deleteDir()
- **Specific File Deletion:** Use sh (or bat on Windows) for fine-grained control:
    - sh 'rm -rf some_directory/'
    - bat 'del /q /s some_other_directory*.txt'
- **Artifact Archiving with Caveats:** While the archiveArtifacts step stores build outputs, use it judiciously. Archiving everything long-term adds to storage usage.

Global Jenkins Configuration

Jenkins offers settings to manage build history and disk usage globally:

1. **Discard Old Builds:** (Manage Jenkins -> Configure System). Configure strategies like:
    - Days to keep builds
    - Max # of builds to keep (per job)

2. **Workspace Cleanup (Plugin):** This optional plugin allows scheduling workspace cleanups on agents.

Cleanup Considerations

- **What's Essential?** Before deleting, determine what build records or artifacts are truly necessary for troubleshooting or historical analysis.
- **External Archival:** For long-term storage needs, consider offloading artifacts to dedicated storage systems (e.g., AWS S3, network shares) and removing them from Jenkins.
- **Post-Build Actions:** Utilize the post section of your pipeline stages for targeted cleanup to keep things tidy as you go:

```
stage('Deploy') {
  // ... Deployment steps
}
post {
  always {
    deleteDir()  // Clean workspace after deploy
  }
}
```

Advanced Techniques

- **Jenkins REST API:** Scripts can interact with the API to manage builds, delete workspaces, and precisely tailor cleanup actions.
- **Shared Libraries:** If you have common cleanup logic, define it in Groovy shared libraries for reuse across pipelines.

Cleanup in Practice

Let's analyze a pipeline you have and consider these questions together:

1. **Storage Impact:** Are there artifacts or files created during the build that could be safely deleted?
2. **Retention Needs:** Do you have business or compliance reasons to keep build history for a certain period? Let's fine-tune Jenkins settings or add a deletion step accordingly.
3. **Externalization:** If a build artifact is essential long-term, could we move it out of Jenkins into a more suitable archival system using a post-build step (e.g., upload to S3)?

Additional Resources

- **Jenkins Wiki - Discard Old Builds**
  https://wiki.jenkins.io/display/JENKINS/Discard+Old+Builds+Plugin
- **Jenkins Wiki - Cleaning up the workspace:**
  https://wiki.jenkins.io/display/JENKINS/Workspace+Cleanup+Plugin
- **Pipeline: Basic Steps plugin** (provides the `deleteDir` step):
  https://www.jenkins.io/doc/book/pipeline/syntax/

Repository Revelations: Cloning Repositories

Let's explore how Jenkins interacts with your source code repositories, pulling your precious code to kick off those all-important pipelines.

Version Control: The Heart of CI/CD

At the core of modern CI/CD pipelines lies a version control system (VCS). This is where Jenkins gets your code to build:

- **Git:** The overwhelmingly popular distributed VCS.
- **Subversion (SVN):** A legacy centralized system, still used in some environments.
- **Mercurial, Perforce....:** Other less common, but sometimes supported VCS options.

Jenkins and Your Repos

The primary way Jenkins gets code is by cloning a repository, creating a local working copy for the build process.

1. Authentication

- **Username/Password:** For basic access, often used in test setups.
- **SSH Keys:** Highly recommended for production due to increased security. Jenkins needs an SSH keypair it can use.
- **API Tokens:** Common with repository hosting services like GitHub, providing controlled access.

2. SCM Configuration in Your Pipeline

Jenkins Pipelines define where and how to obtain code, typically within the `stages` section. Let's look at Git examples:

Declarative Pipeline

```
stage('Checkout') {
    steps {
        git branch: 'main', url: 'https://github.com/myorg/myrepo.git'
    }
```

}

Scripted Pipeline

```
stage('Checkout') {
    steps {
        checkout([
            $class: 'GitSCM',
            branches: [[name: 'main']],
            userRemoteConfigs: [[url:
'https://github.com/myorg/myrepo.git', credentialsId:
'my-github-token']]
        ])
    }
}
```

Considerations

- **Credentials Management:** Jenkins provides a secure vault for storing credentials used to access repositories. Avoid putting them directly into Pipeline scripts!
- **Branch Selection:** The `branch` specifier controls which branches trigger builds and the code checked out.
- **Webhooks (Later Chapter):** A more advanced technique is having your repo provider (GitHub, etc.) notify Jenkins of changes, triggering builds automatically.

Beyond the Basics

- **Submodules:** If your Git repo has submodules, Jenkins can handle them with additional configuration.
- **Shallow Clones:** To save time and space in specific cases, you can use 'shallow clones' fetching limited history.
- **SVN Specifics:** Jenkins has similar steps and setup for Subversion, though specific details will differ.

Security is Key

- **Review your VCS provider's settings:** Use personal access tokens where possible, limit permissions granted.

- **Segregate Credentials:** If using different repos owned by different teams, consider separate credentials per repository to limit the impact if one is compromised.
- **Rotate:** Periodically rotate keys or tokens even if not suspected of being compromised.

Additional Resources

- **Jenkins Git Plugin Documentation:** https://plugins.jenkins.io/git/
- **Jenkins Subversion Plugin:** https://plugins.jenkins.io/subversion/

Practical Challenge

Do you have a Jenkins pipeline in place? If so, let's:

1. **Examine SCM Setup:** How does it fetch code? Are credentials stored securely?
2. **Security Audit:** Could you switch from username/password to SSH keys or API tokens for accessing your repository?
3. **Branching Strategy and Triggers:** Is there a way you could improve how the pipeline reacts to code changes in different branches?

Building Brilliance: Executing the Build Stage

Let's dive headfirst into the stage where your project undergoes its transformation – the "Build" stage.

The Core of Your CI/CD Workflow

The "Build" stage within your pipelines is where:

- **Compilation Happens:** Source code (Java, C#, Python, etc.) is transformed into executable artifacts.
- **Dependencies Are Fetched:** External libraries (via Maven, npm, etc.) are brought in.
- **Packaging:** Files are bundled into deployable units (JARs, WARs, container images, etc.).

Typical Tasks in a Build Stage

1. **Clean Slate (Often):** A `deleteDir()` step or equivalent ensures each build works from a clean workspace.
2. **Tool Invocation:**
   - `mvn package` (Maven)
   - `gradle build` (Gradle)
   - `dotnet build` (.NET)
   - `npm build`, etc. (Node.js and related tools)
3. **Artifact Archival:** Use `archiveArtifacts` to store the output (JARs, WARs) for later use or deployment.

Example: Declarative Java Build Stage

```
stage('Build') {
    steps {
        deleteDir()
        sh 'mvn clean package'
        archiveArtifacts 'target/*.jar'
    }
}
```

Beyond the Basics

- **Static Code Analysis:** Integrate tools like SonarQube, ESLint, or Checkstyle using specific Jenkins plugins.
- **Test Execution (Overlap):** A "Build" stage could run some unit tests. Fuller test suites often get their own "Test" stage.
- **Container Images:** If that's your deployment artifact, use `docker build` steps or the Docker Pipeline plugin.

Key Considerations

1. **Language/Framework Alignment:** The specifics of your build stage depend heavily on your tech stack.
2. **Step Isolation:** Be mindful of tools installed on agents versus those invoked specifically within a stage to prevent conflicts in shared agent environments.
3. **Failure Handling:** Should the entire pipeline fail immediately if the build step fails? You might use `catchError` (Declarative) or `try/catch` (Scripted) for finer control.

Security Focus

- **Dependency Vulnerabilities:** Consider tools that scan your third-party libraries for known security issues.
- **Container Image Scanning:** If you build images, scan them for vulnerabilities (tools like Clair or Trivy).

Optimizing Build Performance

- **Caching:** Maven, npm, etc., have mechanisms to cache dependencies, speeding up subsequent builds if nothing has changed.
- **Incremental Builds:** Certain build systems can be smart about only recompiling what's necessary.
- **Parallelism:** If sensible, some build tasks might be executable in parallel across multiple stages or agents.

Additional Resources

Build Tool Specific Documentation (consider including some for common technology stacks as examples)

- **Maven:** https://maven.apache.org/
- **Gradle:** https://gradle.org/

- **.NET Build Tools:** https://docs.microsoft.com/en-us/dotnet/

Practical Exercise: Analyzing Your Build Stage

Let's dissect a build stage from one of your existing pipelines:

- **Efficiency:** Are there ways to speed it up (caching, parallelism)?
- **Artifacts:** Are you saving the right outputs? Could anything be deleted to save space?
- **Tooling:** Would adding static analysis or security scanning provide valuable insights?

Let's make your build process robust and efficient!

Exploring the DIR Command: A Deep Dive

While the `dir` command might seem simple, it hides valuable functionality for Jenkins pipelines. Let's uncover its depths!

Why 'dir' Matters, Even in CI/CD

1. **Workspace Exploration:** Jenkins builds happen within a workspace. The `dir` step (or `bat 'dir'` on Windows) lets your pipeline list files in the current directory, aiding in troubleshooting.
2. **Targeted Operations:** You can follow up with commands working on a specific subset of files discovered by `dir`.
3. **Cross-Platform Compatibility:** While Linux uses `ls` and Windows primarily has `dir`, Jenkins unifies this within pipelines.

Core Behavior

The main purpose of the `dir` step is to list the contents of a directory, implicitly the current workspace directory. However, it's far more powerful than that!

Example: Finding Java Files (Declarative)

```
stage('Analyze') {
  steps {
      dir('.') {
         script {
             def javaFiles = findFiles(glob: '**/*.java')
             javaFiles.each { file -> println file.path }
         }
      }
   }
}
```

Explanation

- `dir('.') { ... }`: Executes a `dir` step, and the inner script block executes within the workspace directory.
- **findFiles:** A powerful function to locate files based on patterns. The `glob` argument is an Ant-style pattern (e.g., `**/*.java` finds Java files recursively).
- **Iteration:** The code prints the path of each found file.

Advanced Capabilities

Let's step up your `dir` mastery:

1. **File Filtering:** The `findFiles` function supports:
    - `glob`: Ant-style filename patterns (like `*.xml`, `build/**/*.jar`)
    - `regexp`: Regular expressions for complex matching.
2. **Custom Actions:** Within the `dir` block's `script` section, you have Groovy's power. You could:
    - Calculate statistics about the files found.
    - Compress or manipulate files before further pipeline steps.
    - Enforce workspace structure and fail the build if unexpected content exists.
3. **Changing Directory:** The `dir` step takes an optional argument to list a *different* directory within the workspace (e.g., `dir('build/output')`).

Security Note

- **Injecting File Patterns:** If user input ever flows into file patterns for `findFiles`, sanitize it rigorously! Unvalidated input could lead to directory traversal attacks.

Additional Resources

- **Jenkins Pipeline Docs - findFiles:** https://www.jenkins.io/doc/pipeline/steps/pipeline-utility-steps/#findfiles-find-files-in-the-workspace
- **Ant Pattern Syntax:** https://ant.apache.org/manual/dirtasks.html

Practical Scenarios

Let's make this real! Consider these challenges:

- **Cleanup Task:** Write a pipeline stage using `dir` and `deleteDir()` to delete all `.class` files recursively after compilation, keeping the workspace tidy.
- **File Validation:** Create a stage that uses `dir` to find files modified within the last 24 hours within a specific directory and ensure none of them have the word "TODO" anywhere within the file contents.

Harnessing the Power of DIR: Practical Applications

Let's turn your newfound `dir` command knowledge into potent pipeline solutions.

Scenario 1: Enforcing Code Style

Problem: You want to ensure consistent code formatting across a project to improve readability and maintainability.

Solution: Let's introduce a "Code Style Check" stage using `dir` and external tools:

```
stage('Code Style Check') {
    steps {
        dir('.') {
            // Assuming Python and Flake8 as our linter
            sh 'flake8 .'
        }
    }
}
```

Adaptations:

- Swap `flake8 .` with the linter/checker command relevant to your language (eslint for JavaScript, checkstyle for Java, etc.)

Scenario 2: Post-Build Artifact Analysis

Problem: You want a summary of what your build process produced: file counts, sizes, etc.

Solution: A stage employing the power of the `findFiles` function:

```
stage('Build Analysis') {
    steps {
        dir('build/artifacts') {
            def jarFiles = findFiles(glob: '**/*.jar')
            echo "Found ${jarFiles.size()} JAR files"
```

```
            // Calculate total size (Adapt if not using
Java or JARs)
            def totalSize = 0
            jarFiles.each { file -> totalSize +=
file.file.length() }
            echo "Total JAR size: ${totalSize} bytes"
        }
    }
}
```

Scenario 3: Selective Deployment

Problem: You deploy a large application, but usually, only a subset of the produced modules change frequently. You want to deploy only what's changed.

Solution: A stage using timestamps and `dir`:

```
stage('Deploy Modified') {
    steps {
        // Assume last deployment timestamp is stored in a file
        def lastDeployTime =
readFile('lastDeployment.txt').toLong()

        dir('target') {
            def recentlyModified = findFiles(glob: '**/*')
{
                it.file.lastModified() > lastDeployTime
            }
            // ... Logic to deploy 'recentlyModified'
files ...

            // Update timestamp
            writeFile file: 'lastDeployment.txt', text:
"${System.currentTimeMillis()}"
        }
    }
}
```

Important Considerations

- **Performance:** For large workspaces, `findFiles` can become slow. Consider:
    - Pre-build change detection (if your VCS supports it) to narrow down what the pipeline analyzes.
    - Storing metadata to avoid full workspace scans on every build.
- **Cross-Platform:** Ensure file paths and external commands you use within `dir` work on all your agent types (Windows, Linux).

Additional Resources

- **Groovy File Operations:** http://groovy-lang.org/groovy-dev-kit.html#_file_handling

Testing Terrain: Navigating the Test Stage

The Importance of a Dedicated Test Stage

While you might have some tests in your "Build" stage, a distinct "Test" stage offers several compelling advantages:

- **Separation of Concerns:** Decouples the build process (producing artifacts) from their verification.
- **Scalability:** Potentially run different types of tests in parallel on specialized agents.
- **Reporting:** Clear visibility of test results, making it a central point of quality analysis.

Types of Tests Your Pipeline Could Orchestrate

- **Unit Tests:** Focused on individual code components. Fast feedback loop, often the most numerous test type.
- **Integration Tests:** Ensure how different units of your code work together.
- **End-to-End (E2E) Tests:** Simulate user behavior on the complete system. Slower to run, but verify overall functionality.
- **Performance Tests:** Measure response time, throughput, and behavior under load (vital for production readiness!).
- **Security Scans:** Tools analyzing your code or dependencies for known vulnerabilities.

Example: A Multifaceted Test Stage (Declarative)

```
stage('Test') {
    parallel { // Run in parallel if resources allow
        stage('Unit Tests') {
            steps {
                junit '**/target/*.xml'
            }
        }
        stage('Integration') {
            agent { label 'docker-testing' } // Might need specialized agents
            steps {
```

```
                    sh 'docker-compose up -d'
                    sh 'integration-test-runner.sh'
                    sh 'docker-compose down'
                }
            }
        }
    }
}
```

Test Frameworks and Jenkins

Jenkins is agnostic to the testing frameworks you use. Popular choices across languages include:

- **JUnit (Java)**
- **Pytest (Python)**
- **Jest (JavaScript)**
- **RSpec (Ruby)**
- **And many more!**

Jenkins primarily captures and presents test results.

Key Pipeline Steps

1. **Environment Setup:** Preparing databases, containers, or simulators if needed.
2. **Test Execution:** Running your test suites using tools appropriate for your technology (e.g., `mvn test`, `pytest`, `gradle test`).
3. **Result Aggregation:** Jenkins plugins (like 'junit') make test results easily parsable and display them within the build interface.
4. **Quality Gates:** Use `catchError` or conditional logic to potentially fail the build if test failures exceed a threshold.

Additional Considerations

- **Code Coverage:** Integrate tools like JaCoCo (Java) to track how much of your code your tests exercise.
- **Mocking:** For complex integration tests, control external dependencies.
- **Test-Driven Development (TDD):** A philosophy where you write tests *before* production code, covered in a later chapter perhaps?

Resources

- **JUnit Plugin:** https://plugins.jenkins.io/junit/
- **Introduction to Software Testing:**
  https://www.istqb.org/downloads/send/21-ctfl2018/322-ctfl-2018-syllabus-2018-v3-1.html

Practice: Analyzing Your Tests

Let's work together on the following:

1. **Categorize:** Break down the tests in an existing pipeline. Are they primarily unit, integration, etc.?
2. **Opportunities:** Are there test types *missing* that would significantly improve your confidence in changes?
3. **Reporting:** Could you enhance the way test results are presented in Jenkins for a quicker understanding of build health?

Let's make your testing stages robust and informative!

Stage by Stage: Recap and Reinforce

Let's solidify those pipeline concepts with a focused review and provide opportunities to apply them directly to your development processes.

The Purpose of Revisiting

It's easy to get caught up in the details of individual steps. This chapter is about taking a step back and solidifying the big picture of your Jenkins pipelines. We'll aim to:

- **Cement Knowledge:** Ensure the core function of each stage is crystal clear.
- **Identify Connections:** See how stages flow into and depend on each other.
- **Spot Improvement Areas:** Highlight stages that might be inefficient, error-prone, or lacking in quality checks.

Recap: A Typical Pipeline's Journey

1. **Source Acquisition ('Repository Revelations'):**
    - Jenkins fetches your code from version control (Git, SVN, etc.)
2. **Build ('Building Brilliance'):**
    - Code compilation.
    - Dependencies fetched.
    - Artifacts packaged (e.g., JAR, WAR, Docker image).
3. **Test ('Testing Terrain'):**
    - Unit tests to integration tests, potentially in parallel.
    - Quality gates could make the build fail if tests don't pass.
4. **Deploy to Staging:**
    - Built artifacts are sent to a staging environment, a near-production replica.
    - Might involve provisioning infrastructure if needed.
5. **Smoke Tests (Optional):**
    - Basic tests on the deployed staging environment to ensure core functionality is intact.
6. **Approval (Manual or Automated):**
    - A decision point: can the changes move to production? There might be a manual approval or automated checks based on test results, etc.
7. **Deploy to Production:**

- The careful rollout of your changes to the live environment.
- Strategies like blue/green or canary deployments might be in play here.
8. **Monitoring/Observability (Beyond the Pipeline):**
   - While not strictly a Jenkins stage, keeping tabs on the application in production leads to data that might feedback into earlier stages of your pipelines.

Reinforcement Exercises

Now, let's turn this knowledge into action!

Exercise 1: Pipeline Visualization

- **Select a pipeline in your Jenkins environment.**
- **Sketch a diagram:** Don't focus on every step; capture the major stages and their transitions.
- **Review:**
  - Are any stages missing that would add value (more testing, security scanning)?
  - Are there bottlenecks (stages taking very long)?

Exercise 2: Stage Deep-Dive

- **Choose a critical stage from one of your pipelines.**
- **Audit the steps:**
  - Could any steps be combined or made more efficient?
  - Are there clear error handling and failure paths?
  - Can you improve the reporting or visibility of this stage's results?

Exercise 3: The Missing Link

- **Imagine you add a new type of test or analysis** (performance testing, accessibility testing, etc.).
- **Where would it slot into your pipelines?**
  - Would it be a new stage?
  - Are modifications needed to existing stages to accommodate it?

Additional Considerations

- **Branching Strategies & Pipelines:** How do MultiBranch pipelines change the stage concept?

- **Promotions:** If you have the concept of promoting a build artifact through environments, how is this reflected in pipeline stages?

Success Signals: Celebrating Build Success and Analyzing Logs

Let's dive into how Jenkins helps you understand the outcomes of your builds, ensuring success (or guiding you towards fixes).

Why Build Results Matter

Jenkins pipelines work tirelessly, but the results they produce are what truly influences your project. This chapter is about:

- **Swift Feedback:** Quickly knowing if changes are good or have caused problems
- **Root Cause Analysis:** When things go wrong, logs are your guide to the solution
- **Data-Driven Decisions:** Build history informs long-term process improvements

Success! (Hopefully...)

Let's start with the best outcome:

- **Green Light:** Jenkins visually marks a successful build.
- **Artifacts:** The 'Build' stage likely produced the thing you need to deploy (JARs, Docker images, etc.). These are archived by Jenkins.
- **Test Reports:** If you have tests, successful pipelines should have associated test results viewable within Jenkins.
- **Notifications:** Configure Jenkins to send emails, Slack messages, etc., to keep your team in the loop.

When Things Go Wrong

Failures demand attention! Jenkins provides several tools:

- **Red Alert:** Clearly marks failed builds.
- **Stage Identification:** The failed stage is highlighted, narrowing down your search.
- **Console Output:** The heart of troubleshooting. This contains the raw output of the commands that were executed in your pipeline.

Proactive Success: Even in Green Builds

Even successful builds contain a treasure trove of information in their logs:

- **Warnings:** Might not cause failure now, but could be problems later.
- **Timings:** Which stages take longest? Are there optimization gains?
- **Dependency Changes:** Did updates introduce unexpected side effects?

Typical Analysis Workflow (for a Failed Build)

1. **Console Output Starting Point:** Look at the errors near the end of the log for the failing command.
2. **Scroll Backwards:** Trace the error's origin. Was there an earlier setup issue?
3. **Test Failures:** If it's a test failure, the output should pinpoint the broken test.
4. **Reproduce Locally (If Possible):** Can you replicate the error in your development environment? This makes fixing easier.

Improving Log Readability

- **Structured Logging (Consider):** If you control how your application or tests log, outputting in formats like JSON makes it easier to parse with tools later.
- **Log Levels:** Use 'debug' logging for temporary, verbose output, and 'error' to highlight critical problems.
- **Separate Log Files:** For complex pipelines, break output into 'build.log', 'test.log', etc.

Additional Resources

- **Logstash / ELK Stack:** Tools for centralizing and searching logs https://www.elastic.co/logstash
- **Splunk:** Another log analysis platform https://www.splunk.com/

Practice Scenarios

Let's turn these concepts into action. Do you have the following in your Jenkins setup (or could you add them)?

- **Deployment Notifications:** When a successful build reaches a deployment stage, does your team get notified?

- **Warnings as Failure (Optional):** Strict pipelines might fail the build if *any* warnings occur, forcing them to be addressed immediately. Is this right for your project?
- **Timing Analysis:** Do you regularly review logs to see if any stages are becoming disproportionately slow over time?

Let's make your Jenkins builds informative and help you celebrate success with confidence!

Console Chronicles: Understanding Console Output

Let's embark on a journey to decode the mysteries within the Jenkins console output, the raw heart of your pipeline's execution.

The Rosetta Stone of Your Pipelines

The console output is the primary window into what happened during your build. Within its lines lie:

- **Successes:** Commands that completed without error.
- **Failures:** Error messages that illuminate why your build broke.
- **Warnings:** Potential issues that might not cause immediate failure.
- **Informational Output:** Progress indicators, tool/plugin messages, etc.

Making Sense of the Chaos

Raw console output can be overwhelming. Let's develop the skills to find the signal amongst the noise.

- **Structural Clues:**
    - Jenkins prefixes lines with timestamps and [Pipeline] tags to help you see the flow of execution.
    - Stage boundaries can provide a visual separation of where things happen.
- **Error Pinpointing:**
    - Look for words like "error", "failed", or "exception".
    - Stack traces (if present) often point to specific lines of code or configuration.
- **Context Matters:** Lines before and after errors are critical. What led up to the problem?

Example: A Typical Build Snippet

```
[Pipeline] stage (Test) {
    [Pipeline] junit
    Recording test results
    [Pipeline] echo
    Tests completed! 2 failures, 10 passed.
}
```

```
[Pipeline] stage (Deploy to Staging) {
   [Pipeline] sh
   + docker build -t myapp:latest .
   Sending build context to Docker daemon  34.2kB
   ... Docker build output continues ...
}
```

Analysis:

- We can see two distinct stages.
- The 'Test' stage had some failures (investigate further up in the log).
- The 'Deploy to Staging' stage seems to have begun a Docker build process.

Pro Tips

- **Search is Your Friend:** Jenkins' console log has a search bar. Look for specific keywords, command outputs, or file names.
- **'Quiet' Option:** Some Jenkins steps have a 'quiet' mode to reduce non-essential output. Useful when a command is very noisy.
- **Selective Verbosity:** Add more print statements or use echo within your pipeline for intermediate debugging.

Beyond the Basics

- **Real-Time Monitoring:** Jenkins lets you tail the console output as the build is running. This is valuable for long-running builds or to get instant feedback.
- **Remote Logging:** For complex setups, centralize logs using tools like ElasticSearch or Graylog.
- **Pipeline DSL: 'ansiColor'** You can add color to your console output within Declarative Pipelines for better readability (consider a plugin to help manage this).

Additional Resources

- **Jenkins Wiki - Understanding Build Log:**
  https://wiki.jenkins.io/display/JENKINS/Understanding+Jenkins

Replay: Revisiting and Refining Pipelines

Let's explore the power of iteration with Jenkins pipelines. Sometimes, running a build once isn't enough, and the ability to replay and refine is key to a smooth CI/CD process.

Why Replay Matters

- **Troubleshooting:** Is a failure intermittent? Replaying the build helps isolate if the root cause is within your code/configuration or due to external factors.
- **Testing Fixes:** You've changed code to address a bug. Replaying the build verifies if your fix truly worked.
- **Configuration Changes:** Tweaked environment setup or Jenkins settings themselves? Replays confirm everything still works as intended.
- **Audits:** If required, the ability to replay past builds provides traceability and accountability.

Jenkins: Your Replay Control Panel

1. **The Replay Button:** The most basic way. Within a failed build, a 'Replay' button exists. This reruns the pipeline *as-is*.
2. **Replay with Edits (Declarative):** The Replay option in Declarative pipelines lets you modify the pipeline's code directly before relaunching. Excellent for quick experimentation.
3. **Upstream Changes:** If your pipeline is triggered by SCM changes (like a new commit), pushing further changes will generally retrigger the build, incorporating your updates.

Scenarios Where Replay Shines

Let's look at common situations where the ability to replay pipelines is invaluable:

- **Flaky Tests:** Tests that sometimes pass and sometimes fail are a headache. Replay helps you see if the test itself is unreliable or if there's a genuine issue in your code.

- **External Dependencies:** If your build pulls things from the web, network issues could be the culprit. Replaying after a network hiccup should succeed if the problem was transient.
- **Capacity Issues:** Builds failing due to limited resources (disk space, memory) might succeed when replayed on a different agent or at a less busy time.

Advanced Replay Considerations

- **Parameter Replay:** If your pipeline takes parameters, the Replay button usually lets you reuse or modify the previous run's parameters.
- **Artifacts and Workspaces:** By default, Jenkins attempts to reuse the workspace of the original build. Be mindful of this if you *expect* changes, as a replay might not pick up new code.
- **'Replay' Plugins:** There are Jenkins plugins specifically focused on enhanced replay capabilities, potentially allowing you to replay specific stages rather than the whole pipeline.

Proactive Pipelines: Retry Within the Build

Sometimes, you can anticipate temporary failures within your steps. Rather than failing the whole build:

```
stage('Potentially Flaky') {
    retry(3) { // Retry up to 3 times if it fails
        sh 'download-some-resource.sh'
    }
}
```

Additional Resources

- **Jenkins Pipeline Documentation - Retry:**
  https://www.jenkins.io/doc/book/pipeline/syntax/#retry

Practice Time!

Do you have a troublesome pipeline in your Jenkins setup with intermittent issues? Let's try these:

1. **Replication:** Use the Replay button to rerun it several times. Does the failure pattern change?

2. **Targeted Fixes:** Can you add retries to specific steps, or tweak your `Jenkinsfile` to be more resilient to temporary glitches?
3. **Parameter Play:** If your pipeline uses parameters, does changing those on Replay affect the outcome?

Let's transform those unreliable pipelines into robust and repeatable workflows!

Section 5:
GitHub Integration with Jenkins

Setting the Stage: GitHub Integration Essentials, Part 1

Let's lay the groundwork for a powerful alliance between GitHub, the world's most popular Git hosting platform, and your Jenkins CI/CD engine.

Why GitHub and Jenkins Are Better Together

GitHub excels at storing and managing your code, while Jenkins orchestrates the automation surrounding it. Integrating them unlocks:

- **Build on Commit:** Changes pushed to GitHub can automatically trigger builds in Jenkins, streamlining your workflow.
- **Feedback Loop:** Jenkins reports build statuses back to GitHub, so you see success/failure directly on commits and pull requests.
- **Centralized Control:** Jenkins becomes the hub where you manage the pipelines that react to your GitHub repository events.

Prerequisites

- **A GitHub Account:** If you don't have one, head to https://github.com and create one.
- **A Jenkins Installation:** I'm assuming you already have Jenkins up and running.
- **A GitHub Repository:** We'll work with a project you have on GitHub.

Key Concepts

Before we dive into configuration, let's ground ourselves in some essential terminology:

- **Webhooks:** The glue that binds them. GitHub uses webhooks to send notifications (like when code is pushed) to Jenkins.

- **Jenkins Plugins:** Plugins specifically designed for GitHub integration exist; we'll install those.
- **Credentials:** Jenkins needs a way to securely interact with your GitHub account.

Step 1: Installing the GitHub Plugin

1. **Manage Jenkins:** Go to the "Manage Jenkins" section within your Jenkins dashboard.
2. **Plugin Manager:** Select "Plugin Manager" and then the "Available" tab.
3. **Search:** Search for "GitHub plugin" and install it along with its dependencies (like the "Git plugin").
4. **Restart:** Jenkins might require a restart for the plugins to take effect.

Step 2: Generating a GitHub Personal Access Token

1. **GitHub Settings:** On GitHub, go to your settings (top-right icon -> Settings).
2. **Developer Settings:** Navigate to "Developer settings" on the left-hand sidebar.
3. **Personal Access Tokens:** Select "Personal access tokens" and click "Generate new token".
4. **Permissions (Important):** Grant the token the necessary permissions (often just `repo` is needed for basic integration). Be cautious with excessive permissions!
5. **Copy It:** Copy your newly generated token and store it securely (you won't be able to see it again after leaving this page).

Step 3: Adding Credentials to Jenkins

1. **Credentials Management:** Depending on your Jenkins version, this will either be in the main "Manage Jenkins" area or accessible from the dashboard.
2. **Domains (May Vary):** If your Jenkins has domains, you likely want to add credentials to the "Global" domain.
3. **Add Credentials:** Click "Add Credentials."
4. **Kind:** Select "Username with password".
5. **Username:** Usually, this is your GitHub username.
6. **Password:** Paste your Personal Access Token.
7. **Description:** A helpful description like "GitHub Integration Token".

Additional Resources

- **GitHub Plugin Documentation:** https://plugins.jenkins.io/github/

Check Your Understanding

To make sure we're on the same page:

- **Terminology:** Can you explain what a webhook is in the context of Jenkins-GitHub integration?
- **Security:** Why is it a better practice to use a Personal Access Token rather than your main GitHub password in Jenkins?

In Part 2, we'll configure your first Jenkins pipeline to be triggered by GitHub events and see this integration in action!

Preparing Your GitHub Environment: GitHub Integration Essentials, Part 2

Let's pick up where we left off and prepare your GitHub repository to talk to Jenkins. With the groundwork laid in Part 1, we're now ready to make the connection!

Step 4: Configuring a GitHub Webhook

1. **Repository Settings:** Navigate to the GitHub repository you want to integrate with Jenkins. Click on "Settings."
2. **Webhooks:** In the sidebar, select "Webhooks" and then click the "Add webhook" button.
3. **Payload URL:** This is where Jenkins listens for events. It will look something like: `http://<your-jenkins-url>/github-webhook/`. Importantly, your Jenkins needs to be reachable from the public internet for this to work.
4. **Content Type:** Choose "application/json".
5. **Which Events?** "Just the push event" is a common start for triggering builds. You can select more later (pull requests, etc.).
6. **Active:** Ensure the webhook is marked as Active.

Important: Firewalls and Security

- If your Jenkins is behind a firewall, you may need to configure port forwarding or expose it differently to make it accessible for GitHub's webhook calls.
- Advanced setups can involve a tunnel (like `ngrok`) during development.
- For production, a publicly resolvable domain for your Jenkins instance is strongly recommended.

Step 5: Creating Your First Jenkins Pipeline

We'll keep the Jenkins side simple for now:

1. **New Item:** Create a new item in Jenkins and choose either "Freestyle project" or "Pipeline" as the project type. Give it a name.
2. **Pipeline Script (If Pipeline Project):**

```
node {
    stage('Basic Checkout') {
```

```
            git url:
'https://github.com/<your-username>/<your-repo>.git'
        }
    }
}
```

- Replace `<your-username>` and `<your-repo>` accordingly.
3. **Source Code Management:** Select "GitHub" and connect it to your project if you haven't already. Jenkins might auto-discover your webhook if configured earlier.

The Moment of Truth: Test It!

Make a small change to any file in your GitHub repository and push the commit. With any luck, this should trigger a build in your Jenkins!

Troubleshooting 101

- **Jenkins Build Log:** Did the build trigger at all? The log will indicate if the GitHub event was received.
- **GitHub Webhook Delivery:** On your GitHub webhook settings page, it shows recent delivery attempts and their outcomes.
- **Firewalls:** Double-check if anything is blocking Jenkins from being reached.

Additional Considerations

- **Credentials:** In production setups, avoid putting credentials directly in your `Jenkinsfile`. Use Jenkins' built-in Credentials system that we configured earlier.
- **Branch Specifiers:** You can configure your Jenkins job to react only to changes on specific branches (e.g., your 'main' branch).

Resources

- **GitHub Webhooks Documentation:**
  https://docs.github.com/en/developers/webhooks-and-events/webhooks

Exercises

- **Get Specific:** Can you modify the pipeline to checkout a specific branch of your repository?

- **Status Updates:** There's a GitHub plugin specifically for sending build status updates back to GitHub. Experiment with installing and using it so you can see success/failure on your commits.

Let's get those builds flowing from GitHub to Jenkins!

Polling SCM: Navigating Source Code Management, Part 1

Let's explore an alternative mode of Jenkins-GitHub interaction. While webhooks offer near real-time reaction, there are scenarios where polling (Jenkins asking for changes) is the right tool for the job.

When Webhooks Might Not Be Ideal

- **Behind Strict Firewalls:** If your Jenkins is entirely inaccessible to the outside world, it can't receive GitHub's webhook notifications.
- **Infrequent Changes:** Webhooks generate a bit of network overhead for each event. If your repository isn't super active, polling on a schedule could be more efficient.
- **Legacy Systems:** Sometimes, you might be integrating with a source control system that simply doesn't support webhooks.

How SCM Polling Works

1. **Schedule:** You configure a Jenkins job to poll your GitHub repository on a schedule (e.g., every 15 minutes).
2. **Jenkins Asks:** Jenkins reaches out to GitHub and asks, "Have there been any changes to the code since the last time I checked?"
3. **Fetch If Changes:** If GitHub says "yes," Jenkins then pulls down the latest code.

Configuring Polling in Your Jenkins Pipeline

Let's modify the pipeline from the previous chapter. Assuming you are using a "Pipeline" project type:

```
node {
    git url: 'https://github.com/<your-username>/<your-repo>.git',
poll: true // Ask for changes

    // Optionally specify branch:
    // git ... , branch: 'main'

    // ... Your build steps go here ...
}
```

- **Important:** Remove any GitHub webhook configuration from the job and from the GitHub repository settings if you had set that up earlier.

Setting the Polling Schedule

There are a few ways to set the schedule:

1. **Build Triggers Section:** Look for "Poll SCM" in your project configuration.
2. **H Syntax (Cron-Like):** You can express schedules like "Poll every 10 minutes" using a special syntax within the `poll: true` option. A common example is H/10 * * * *

Trade-Offs: Webhooks vs. Polling

Feature	Webhooks	Polling
Change Latency	Near real-time	Delay based on schedule
Network Traffic	Event-driven (lower if infrequent)	Potential for more overhead
Firewall Hassle	Jenkins needs to be publicly exposed	Can work with internal-only Jenkins

Resources

- **Jenkins SCM Polling:** https://www.jenkins.io/doc/book/pipeline/syntax/#triggers
- **H Syntax for Scheduling:** https://www.jenkins.io/doc/book/pipeline/syntax/#triggers

Practice Time

- **Conversion:** Do you have a pipeline currently using webhooks? Try converting it to use polling instead. Observe the timing differences in when builds trigger.
- **Pros and Cons Exercise:** Think of a few more scenarios (beyond those mentioned) where polling might be explicitly better than webhooks, and vice versa.

Efficiency Considerations

- SCM polling can lead to lots of builds where nothing has changed.
- Some Jenkins plugins provide advanced polling options like only triggering if changes are found in certain file paths, which can improve efficiency. Let's discuss this more in Part 2 of this exploration!

Fine-Tuning SCM: Maximizing Source Code Management, Part 2

Let's dive into streamlining how Jenkins interacts with your GitHub repositories for optimized CI/CD workflows.

Beyond the Basics of Polling

In the previous chapter, we introduced polling as an alternative to webhooks. Here's how we can refine it:

- **Quiet Periods:** Some plugins allow you to skip polling if there have been no changes for a certain amount of time, preventing needless builds overnight or on weekends.
- **Path Filtering:** If your project is large, consider configuring the polling mechanism to consider changes *only within relevant directories* (this depends on plugin capabilities).
- **Lightweight Polling:** Some SCM systems offer less intensive checks to see if *anything* has changed, followed by a more thorough fetch only if needed.

Branch Management Strategies with Polling

- **Poll Everything:** You can configure your Jenkins pipeline to poll *all branches* of your repository. Strategies exist to differentiate the behavior of the pipeline based on the branch it detects.
- **Dedicated Pipelines per Branch:** A more structured approach is separate Jenkins pipelines for crucial branches (main, release branches), each potentially polling on a different schedule.

Git-Specific Optimizations

- **Shallow Clones:** If you don't need the full commit history during the build, a 'shallow clone' fetches only the latest commits, saving bandwidth.
- **Sparse Checkouts:** For big repos, this lets you check out only subdirectories relevant to your build.
- **Submodules:** If your project has Git submodules, Jenkins' handling of these can be customized for efficiency.

Caveat: Polling Granularity Depends on Plugins

The specific optimizations mentioned above often rely on the features of your chosen Git/GitHub plugin in Jenkins.

Example: Fine-Tuning with the GitHub Plugin (Assuming you're using the popular GitHub plugin)

1. **Branch Filtering:** Within the SCM configuration in your pipeline, look for options to include or exclude specific branches from polling.
2. **Advanced Polling:** Some plugins may provide a separate trigger type in your job configuration specifically for advanced polling.

The Case for Hybrid: Webhooks + Polling

- **Webhooks for Core Flow:** Rely on webhooks for your primary development branches (main, etc.) to get immediate feedback.
- **Polling as a Backstop:** Set up a nightly polling job that sweeps all branches. This could catch things like a forgotten feature branch that wasn't integrated or long-running branches that fell out of sync.

Additional Resources

- **Git SCM Plugin (General):** https://plugins.jenkins.io/git/
- **GitHub Plugin (Specific Optimizations):** https://plugins.jenkins.io/github/

Practical Challenge

Let's make your setup more efficient. Consider the following:

1. **Project Size and Activity:** Do you have a very large repository or one with very infrequent commits? If so, optimizing polling becomes more important.
2. **Plugin Investigation:** Based on your current SCM-related Jenkins plugins, explore if they offer advanced polling features (check official plugin documentation).
3. **Is a Hybrid Approach Right for You?** Could you benefit from fast webhook reactions on most branches, but with a less frequent polling job as a safeguard?

Section 6:
Navigating MultiBranch Pipelines

Branching Out: Understanding Branches

Let's embark on a journey into the realm of branches and how they fundamentally shape your development workflows, especially when we bring Jenkins into the picture.

Why Branches Matter

Branches in version control systems (like Git) are at the heart of collaborative and agile software development. Think of them as parallel universes where you can:

1. **Isolate Changes:** Experiment with new features or bug fixes without destabilizing your main codebase.
2. **Collaborate Fearlessly:** Multiple developers can work on different features concurrently, merging their branches when the work is ready.
3. **Versioning and Rollback:** Branches can preserve snapshots of your project's history. If needed, you can revert to older states.

Common Branching Strategies

- **Main/Trunk-Based:** A central "main" or "trunk" branch represents your production-ready code. Short-lived feature branches merge back into this main branch.
- **Gitflow:** A more structured system with branches for development, hotfixes, releases, and features.
- **GitHub Flow:** A lightweight cousin of Gitflow, centered around feature branches and pull requests.

Branching and CI/CD: The Jenkins Connection

This is where things get really interesting. Jenkins can:

- **React to Branch Changes:** Jenkins can be aware of branches in your repository and execute different processes depending on the branch.

- **Testing in Isolation:** Feature branches might have their own pipelines for testing and validation before being merged back into the main branch.
- **Release Management:** Jenkins can help orchestrate the flow of code from release branches through staging environments and ultimately into production.

Key Git Concepts (Quick Refresher)

- **Commits:** A snapshot of changes at a point in time.
- **Branches:** A lightweight pointer to a specific commit. Branches diverge as new commits are made.
- **Merging:** Combining the changes from one branch into another.
- **Pull Requests (GitHub/GitLab):** A mechanism to propose and review changes from a branch before merging them.

Branching Considerations for Your Jenkins Setup

1. **How Does Your Team Use Branches?** The way you configure Jenkins pipelines should align with your team's chosen branching model.
2. **Build Frequency vs. Thoroughness:** Do you want every commit on every branch to trigger a build, or are builds focused on key branches?
3. **Reporting and Visibility:** How will you keep track of builds happening across different branches?

Resources

- **Git Branching (Atlassian Doc):**
  https://www.atlassian.com/git/tutorials/using-branches
- **Popular Branching Models:**
  https://www.atlassian.com/git/tutorials/comparing-workflows

Practice: Visualizing Your Branches

- **Tools:** Git clients (command-line or GUI) often have ways to display a visual representation of your project's branches and how they relate.
- **Reflection:** Take a look at this visualization for your current project. Does it align with your team's intended branching workflow?

In the next chapter, we'll dive into how Jenkins' MultiBranch pipelines supercharge your ability to manage builds across the branches of your projects!

MultiBranch Pipeline Mastery: Setup Essentials, Part 1

Let's unlock the power of Jenkins MultiBranch pipelines. Get ready to streamline your workflows as Jenkins dynamically discovers, manages, and builds your various branches!

Prerequisites

- **Jenkins Installation:** I'm assuming you have a functional Jenkins instance ready to go.
- **GitHub Project (Ideally):** We'll get the most out of this with a GitHub project having a few different branches.
- **Required Plugins:** Make sure you have the following Jenkins plugins installed (they usually come bundled by default):
    - Git plugin
    - GitHub Branch Source plugin (if using GitHub)

What Makes MultiBranch Pipelines Special

1. **Automatic Branch Discovery:** Most basic Jenkins pipelines need to be explicitly configured for a branch. MultiBranch Pipelines can scan your repository and find relevant branches.
2. **Builds per Branch:** They enable you to define a Jenkinsfile that governs what happens when code changes on any of your branches.
3. **Webhooks, But Still Flexible:** While designed to work well with webhooks, MultiBranch pipelines can also be manually triggered or set on schedules.

Step 1: Creating a MultiBranch Pipeline Job

1. **New Item:** Click on "New Item" in your Jenkins dashboard.
2. **Choose the Type:** Select "MultiBranch Pipeline" as the project type, and give it a descriptive name.

Step 2: Configuring Source Control

1. **Branch Sources:** Under "Branch Sources," add a source. Most commonly, you'll choose "GitHub" here.

2. **Credentials:** You'll likely need to provide your Jenkins with the credentials needed to connect to your GitHub account (we covered this in earlier chapters).
3. **Owner:** This is your GitHub account or organization name.
4. **Repository:** Select the repository you want Jenkins to monitor.

Step 3: The Scan Trigger (How It Finds Branches)

- **Webhooks:** When you save the configuration, Jenkins will (if configured correctly) auto-generate a webhook URL for you to paste into your GitHub repository settings. This is the ideal mode for real-time reaction to branch changes.
- **Periodic Scan:** If you can't use webhooks, you can tell Jenkins to scan your repository for changes on a schedule (e.g., every 15 minutes).

Step 4: The Magic Ingredient – Your Jenkinsfile

MultiBranch pipelines look for a file named `Jenkinsfile` **in the root of your repository**. This file has the usual Declarative or Scripted Pipeline syntax we've explored previously.

Example Jenkinsfile (Declarative Style)

```
pipeline {

    agent any


    stages {

        stage('Test') {

            steps {

                sh 'mvn test'

            }

        }

    }

}
```

Important! This `Jenkinsfile` will be applied by Jenkins if it finds branches.

Let's Build!

Save your configuration. Here's what happens next:

1. **Initial Scan:** Jenkins will scan your repo and detect branches.
2. **Builds Triggered:** If it finds new branches with changes and a `Jenkinsfile`, it will start build jobs specifically for those branches.
3. **Jenkins UI Updates:** Your Jenkins dashboard will show separate build entries for each active branch it's managing.

Resources

- **Jenkins MultiBranch Pipeline Tutorial:** https://www.jenkins.io/doc/book/pipeline/multibranch/

Challenges

Let's troubleshoot if things don't work right away:

- **Webhook Delivery Failed?** Check your GitHub repo's webhook settings and recent delivery attempts.
- **Build Errors?** Inspect the build logs for the specific branches that Jenkins discovers. Is your `Jenkinsfile` correct?

In Part 2, we'll explore how to customize behaviors for different branches, index sources other than GitHub, and harness the full power of MultiBranch Pipelines!

MultiBranch Pipeline Mastery: Setup Essentials, Part 2

Let's continue our deep dive into Jenkins MultiBranch Pipelines and how they can reshape your CI/CD processes.

Controlling Behavior Based on Branches

While it's powerful to have a unified Jenkinsfile for core actions, some branches need special treatment:

- **Example:** Your 'develop' branch might run basic tests, while your 'release' branches might run additional security or compliance checks.

Technique 1: Branch-Specific Logic in Your Jenkinsfile

Within your Jenkinsfile, you have access to an environment variable called BRANCH_NAME

```
pipeline {
    agent any
    stages {
        stage('Branch Aware Test') {
            when { branch 'main' }
            steps {
                sh 'mvn test'
                sh 'mvn security-scan' // Additional for 'main'
            }
        }
    }
}
```

Technique 2: Separate Jenkinsfiles (Rare)

In less common scenarios, you could have different Jenkinsfile files placed in specific branch directories within your project, but this often leads to duplication.

Source Control Beyond GitHub

While we've focused on GitHub, MultiBranch Pipelines can work with other Git providers or even Subversion (SVN) repositories. You'd choose the appropriate source control plugin during setup.

Build Strategies

Found within the configuration of your MultiBranch Pipeline project:

- **Discard Old Items:** Allows you to discard builds for stale branches, keeping things tidy.
- **Periodic Build Triggers:** Even with webhooks, you might force periodic scans if you are concerned about missed webhook events.
- **Suppress Automatic SCM Triggering:** Turns off automatic builds for branch changes, essentially disabling the MultiBranch aspect, if desired.

Pro Tip: Indexing and Performance

Indexing (where Jenkins examines branches) can be resource-intensive for huge repositories. Some optimization features exist:

- **Lightweight Checkout (when possible):** Don't fetch a full clone if Jenkins only needs branch metadata.
- **Exclude Branches:** Use regular expression patterns to ignore branches you never intend to build on.

Jenkins UI Tips

1. **Project View:** Your Jenkins main view will now showcase your MultiBranch project and its branch statuses individually.
2. **Branch Filtering:** Often, there's a UI control to filter visible branches in the project view.
3. **Orphaned Items:** Sometimes Jenkins discovers branches but loses track of them later (deleted on GitHub, etc.). These might need manual removal from Jenkins.

Additional Features to Explore (Beyond the Essentials)

- **Status Reporting:** Some plugins send richer status updates back to GitHub (beyond basic success/failure), enhancing the developer experience.
- **Job DSL:** MultiBranch pipelines can be defined using Jenkins' Job DSL, allowing infrastructure-as-code approaches.

Resources

- **Jenkins Blog on MultiBranch Pipelines:**
  https://www.jenkins.io/blog/2015/12/03/pipeline-as-code-with-multibranch-workflows-in-jenkins/

Practice: Branching Hygiene

A well-functioning MultiBranch CI/CD setup depends on a good branching strategy in your development team. Do you have the following in place?

- **Naming Conventions:** Are branches named such that Jenkins could make some assumptions about them (if desired)?
- **Lifecycle:** Is there a clear process for short-lived feature branches vs. longer-lived release branches?

Section 7:
Harnessing the Power of Parameterized Pipelines

Parameterized Pipelines Unveiled: An Introduction

Let's demystify the world of Parameterized Pipelines and how they add flexibility to your Jenkins workflows.

Why Parameters Matter

Up until now, our pipelines have been quite rigid. They do the same thing every time. Parameters inject the ability to:

- **Customize Builds:** Run the same pipeline but build a different branch, target a different environment, etc.
- **User Input:** Allow a user to provide choices when triggering a build
- **Reusability:** A single pipeline can serve a wider range of use cases

How Parameters Are Defined (Declarative Pipeline Example)

```
pipeline {
    agent any
    parameters {
        string(name: 'DEPLOY_ENVIRONMENT', defaultValue: 'staging', description: 'Which environment to deploy to?')
        booleanParam(name: 'RUN_SMOKE_TESTS', defaultValue: true, description: 'Run post-deployment smoke tests?')
    }
    stages {
        // ... Your build stages that can use the parameters ...
    }
```

}

- **The 'parameters' Block:** This is where you define the parameters your pipeline accepts.
- **Types:** Common types include strings (text), booleans (true/false), choices, and more.
- **Defaults and Descriptions:** Make your pipeline user-friendly!

Accessing Parameters within Your Pipeline

Inside your `stages`, you access parameters using the `params` object:

```
stage('Deployment') {
    steps {
        echo "Deploying to environment: ${params.DEPLOY_ENVIRONMENT}"
        sh './deploy.sh ${params.DEPLOY_ENVIRONMENT}'
    }
}
```

Triggering Builds with Parameters

- **"Build with Parameters" Option:** If your job is configured to have parameters, Jenkins will present a form when you manually trigger a build.
- **API and CLI Tools:** Build triggering with parameters can be done through the Jenkins API or command-line tools for automation.

Examples to Illustrate the Power

- **Scenario 1: Test Matrix**
    - Parameter: Browser Type (Chrome, Firefox, Edge)
    - Your test stage runs tests, but the browser to use is driven by the parameter.
- **Scenario 2: Artifact Selection**
    - Parameter: A list of build numbers from a previous job
    - The pipeline retrieves and deploys the artifact corresponding to the build number chosen
- **Scenario 3: Release Approval**
    - Parameter: Approve Deployment (Boolean)

○ The pipeline pauses and waits for manual input from an authorized user before proceeding with deployment to production.

Additional Considerations

- **Pipeline Script vs. UI:** For complex parameter definitions and logic, the Scripted Pipeline syntax can offer more power than the Declarative UI elements.
- **Validation:** You can add some basic input validation to your parameters.
- **Jenkins Plugins:** Plugins extend parameter capabilities, providing things like secure password parameters, file selection parameters, and more.

Resources

- **Jenkins Wiki - Parameters:** https://wiki.jenkins.io/display/JENKINS/Parameterized+Build
- **Parameterized Trigger Plugin** (Useful for chaining parameterized builds): https://plugins.jenkins.io/parameterized-trigger/

Practice: Parameterize Something!

Think of a Jenkins pipeline you already have. Answer the following:

1. **What Task Could be Parameterized?** Could a choice of environment, a version number, or a configuration setting be a parameter?
2. **Impact:** How would this improve the pipeline's reusability or flexibility?

Putting Theory into Practice: Live Demonstration

Let's get hands-on and solidify your understanding of parameterized pipelines through a guided demonstration.

Prerequisites

- **Jenkins Instance:** I assume you already have a Jenkins installation up and running.
- **Basic Pipeline Knowledge:** You should be comfortable with the core concepts of creating a Jenkins job and defining a basic `Jenkinsfile` with stages.

Demonstration Scenario: Customizable Deployment

Our goal is to build a parameterized Jenkins pipeline that performs the following:

1. **Deploys an Application:** We'll keep the deployment steps generic for the sake of this demo.
2. **Environment Selection:** The pipeline will take a parameter to determine the target environment (e.g., dev, staging, production).
3. **Optional Smoke Tests:** A checkbox will control whether to run a suite of post-deployment smoke tests.

Step 1: Creating a New Pipeline Job

1. In Jenkins, click on "New Item."
2. Choose "Pipeline" as the project type and give it a descriptive name (like "parameterized-deployment-demo").

Step 2: Defining the Parameters

1. Under the "Pipeline" section, tick the checkbox that says, "This project is parameterized."
2. **Add a String Parameter:**
    - Name: `target_environment`
    - Default Value: `staging`
    - Description: "The environment to deploy into (dev, staging, prod)"
3. **Add a Boolean Parameter:**

- Name: `run_smoke_tests`
- Default Value: Checked
- Description: "If selected, run smoke tests after deployment"

Step 3: Crafting the Jenkinsfile

```
pipeline {
    agent any
    parameters {
        string(name: 'target_environment', defaultValue: 'staging', description: 'The environment to deploy into (dev, staging, prod)')
        booleanParam(name: 'run_smoke_tests', defaultValue: true, description: 'If selected, run smoke tests after deployment')
    }
    stages {
        stage('Deploy') {
            steps {
                echo "Deploying application to ${params.target_environment}"
                // ... (Your deployment logic here, potentially environment-specific)...
            }
        }
        stage('Smoke Tests') {
            when { expression { params.run_smoke_tests } } // Only runs if checked
            steps {
                echo "Executing smoke tests"
                // ... (Your smoke test commands) ...
            }
        }
    }
}
```

Step 4: Test Drive!

1. Save your pipeline configuration.
2. Click "Build with Parameters." You should see a form representing the parameters we defined.

3. Try these variations:
    - Leave defaults, click "Build."
    - Change `target_environment` to 'dev', run again.
    - Uncheck `run_smoke_tests` and run a third time.

Step 5: Inspecting the Output

Examine the console output of each build run. Notice how:

- The deployment messages reflect the chosen environment.
- The 'Smoke Tests' stage executes conditionally.

Key Takeaways

- **User-Facing:** Your parameterized build is easy to trigger by your team members.
- **Jenkinsfile Centric:** The logic controlling your parameters resides within your pipeline script.
- **Conditional Execution:** You saw how parameters can control the very flow of your pipeline's stages.

Extra Challenges (to do on your own):

- **Deployment Differences:** Could you modify the 'Deploy' stage to actually have different deployment steps based on the `target_environment`?
- **More Parameter Types:** Experiment with the 'choice' parameter type to present a dropdown list to the user.

Boolean Parameters Demystified, Part 1

Let's illuminate the world of Boolean parameters, those simple yet powerful flags that can steer the behavior of your Jenkins pipelines.

True or False: The Power of Choice

Boolean parameters are all about decisions within your pipelines. They essentially represent yes/no choices with the following characteristics:

- **User Input:** Presented as checkboxes when a user triggers a build.
- **Conditional Logic:** Inside your pipeline, you use their values to dictate which blocks of code should or should not execute.
- **Typical Use Cases:**
    - Optional features ("Run additional security scan?")
    - Deployment approvals ("Deploy to production?")
    - Environment-specific toggles: ("Perform database cleanup?")

Defining a Boolean Parameter (Declarative)

```
pipeline {
    parameters {
        booleanParam(name: 'PUBLISH_DOCS', defaultValue: false, description: 'Should documentation be published?')
    }
    // ... rest of your pipeline ...
}
```

Let's break it down:

- **booleanParam:** This tells Jenkins the parameter type.
- **name:** The name you'll use to reference this (i.e., `params.PUBLISH_DOCS`)
- **defaultValue:** What it's set to if the user doesn't check the box.
- **description:** Helps your users understand the parameter's purpose.

Using Boolean Parameters for Control Flow

The most common way to use Booleans is within when conditions in your stages:

```
stage('Publish Documentation (Optional)') {
```

```
        when { expression { params.PUBLISH_DOCS } }
        steps {
            // Your documentation publishing steps here
        }
    }
```

- **when:** This stage will only execute if PUBLISH_DOCS is 'true'.

More Examples

- **Testing Variation**

```
stage('Extra Tests') {
    when {
        branch 'production'
        expression { params.RUN_STRESS_TESTS }
    }
    steps {
        // ...
    }
}
```

This stage would run more intense tests but only on the 'production' branch and when the RUN_STRESS_TESTS parameter is checked.

Advanced Tip: Combining Booleans

You can use boolean operators (&& - AND, || - OR, ! - NOT) within your when expressions for complex logic.

Boolean Parameters in Action

Let's enhance our deployment demo from the previous chapter:

```
// ...other parameters...
booleanParam(name: 'APPROVE_PRODUCTION', defaultValue: false, description: 'Approve deployment to production')

stage('Deploy to Production') {
    when { expression { params.target_environment == 'prod' && params.APPROVE_PRODUCTION } }
```

```
    steps {
        // ... deployment steps specific to production ...
    }
}
```

Now, production deployment has a safeguard controlled by a parameter.

Additional Considerations

- **Groovy Power:** For complex logic, Scripted Pipelines might offer more flexibility than Declarative Boolean parameter usage.
- **Validation:** Jenkins offers basic input validation for your parameters.

Resources

- **Jenkins Wiki on Parameters:**
  https://wiki.jenkins.io/display/JENKINS/Parameterized+Build

Challenges

1. **Your Pipeline:** Think about a pipeline you have. Is there a task or feature that would be a good candidate for being controlled by a Boolean parameter?
2. **Conditional Cleanup:** Could you add a stage to a pipeline that performs cleanup tasks, but only runs under certain conditions set by Boolean parameters?

Boolean Parameters Demystified, Part 2

Let's continue our exploration of Boolean parameters and how they can add flexibility and decision-making to your Jenkins pipelines!

Beyond the Basics

In Part 1, we covered the fundamentals. Now, let's look at some more nuanced use cases and techniques.

Use Case 1: Deployment Gates

```
stage('Deploy to Staging') {
    // ... deployment logic ...
}
stage('Deploy to Production') {
    input {
        message 'Approve deployment to production?'
        ok 'Yes'
        parameters {
            booleanParam(name: 'DEPLOY_APPROVED', defaultValue: false, description: '')
        }
    }
    when { expression { params.DEPLOY_APPROVED } }
    // ... production deployment logic ...
}
```

- **The `input` Step:** This pauses your pipeline and asks the user for confirmation before proceeding.
- **Approval Parameter:** The input step introduces a temporary Boolean parameter.

Use Case 2: Optional, Time-Intensive Tasks

```
stage('Long-Running Compliance Checks') {
    when {
        environment name: 'production', value: 'true'
        expression { params.ENABLE_COMPLIANCE }
    }
    // ... time-consuming checks here ...
```

}

- **Environment-Aware:** Using the environment directive, this stage runs only on production and when the parameter is selected.

Groovy Enhancement: Default Values Based on Logic

Scripted Pipelines let you calculate default parameter values:

```
node {
    properties([
        parameters([
            booleanParam(name: 'RUN_INTEGRATION_TESTS', defaultValue: hasBranchChanges(), description: 'Run integration tests (auto-calculated default)')
        ])
    ])
    // ...
}


// Helper function
def hasBranchChanges() {
    // Logic to determine if the current branch has significant code changes...
    return true  // Or false, based on your calculation
}
```

- **Dynamic Defaults:** The defaultValue is determined when the build starts, giving you much more power than static defaults.

Security Considerations

- **Sensitive Parameters:** Be mindful of what you name your Boolean parameters. Avoid exposing internal processes or technology choices in the parameter names visible to users.
- **input Step Protection:** The input step is a potential place to inject malicious activity. Treat user input with caution, especially if it influences downstream steps in your pipeline.

Troubleshooting Tips

- **Inspect Parameter Values:** Within your pipeline script, echo the values of your Boolean parameters to verify they are what you expect.
- **Console Output:** Carefully examine the build's console output, especially any stages controlled by Booleans.

Pro Tip: Combining with Other Parameters

Boolean parameters are at their most potent when combined with other parameter types. Imagine:

- A String parameter to select an environment.
- A Boolean to enable/disable a special cleanup process for that environment.

Additional Resources

- **Jenkins input Step Documentation:**
  https://www.jenkins.io/doc/book/pipeline/syntax/#input

Practice: Parameterize It!

Consider these scenarios. Could the introduction of Boolean parameters improve these pipelines?

- **Backup:** A pipeline that backs up a database. Do you always need the backup, or could it be optional?
- **Notifications:** Should failure notifications be sent to different channels (email, Slack, etc.) based on the criticality configured by the user?

String Parameters: Customizing Pipeline Inputs

Let's dive into the realm of String parameters, where pipelines become adaptable to the text-based inputs your users provide!

Why Strings Matter

While Booleans give us 'yes/no' choices, String parameters empower users to inject specific values:

- **Deployment Targets:** "dev", "test", "production"
- **Configuration Settings:** Custom URLs, API keys (use with caution!), feature toggle names
- **Version Control:** Branch names, Git commit hashes
- **Artifact Selection:** Build numbers or labels from previous pipeline runs

Defining a String Parameter (Declarative)

```
pipeline {
    parameters {
        string(name: 'MESSAGE', defaultValue: 'Hello!', description: 'A friendly message')
    }
    // ... your pipeline stages ...
}
```

- **Key Differences (vs. Boolean):**
    - We use `string` to define the parameter type.
    - `defaultValue` is now a text value.

Using String Parameters

Just like other parameter types, you reference them using `params.YOUR_PARAMETER_NAME`:

```
stage('Display Input') {
    steps {
        echo "The provided message was: ${params.MESSAGE}"
    }
```

}

Example: Branch Build

```
parameters {
    string(name: 'SOURCE_BRANCH', defaultValue: 'main',
description: 'Which branch to build')
}
stage('Checkout') {
    steps {
        git branch: "${params.SOURCE_BRANCH}", url:
'https://github.com/your-org/your-repo.git'
    }
}
```

Advanced Features

- **Validation:** Jenkins allows basic validation rules for String parameters (e.g., regular expressions to enforce format).
- **Groovy Power:** In Scripted Pipelines, you can dynamically generate the default value of a String parameter based on other logic.

String Parameters in Action: Artifact Deployment

Let's enhance our deployment pipeline:

```
parameters {
    string(name: 'ARTIFACT_VERSION', defaultValue: '',
description: 'Version or build ID of the artifact to
deploy')
    // ... (other parameters) ...
}
stage('Deploy') {
    steps {
        // Deployment logic, potentially using
${params.ARTIFACT_VERSION}
    }
}
```

Now, users can specify exactly which artifact they want to be deployed.

Security Considerations

- **Input Sanitization:** If a String parameter influences code execution flows, treat its value as potentially unsafe. Implement input sanitization or restrictions as needed.
- **Secrets:** While String parameters can be tempting for secrets, it's generally best practice to use Jenkins' built-in Credentials system for sensitive data.

Resources

- **Jenkins Wiki on the 'string' Parameter**
  https://plugins.jenkins.io/parameterized-trigger/

Practice: String-ify It!

Consider these scenarios. Where could String parameters enhance your pipelines?

1. **File Selection:** A pipeline processing files. Could the filename be a parameter?
2. **Remote Server Configuration:** If a pipeline deploys to multiple environments, could the server hostname or IP address be a parameter?

Let's Design! Picking one of those scenarios, or one of your own, describe how a String parameter would improve it.

Parameter Tracking: Monitoring Parameter Usage

Let's explore how to gain visibility into the parameter choices that drive your Jenkins pipelines, a key aspect in understanding their behavior.

Why Tracking Matters

When your pipelines are parameterized, each build execution is like a unique journey with decisions made along the way. Parameter tracking helps you answer:

- **Troubleshooting:** When a build fails, were the provided parameter values the culprit?
- **Auditing:** Who triggered a build, and what choices did they make?
- **Usage Patterns:** Are there frequently used parameter combinations you should optimize for?

Method 1: Build Parameters Section

Every Jenkins build has a dedicated "Parameters" link in its sidebar. This provides the most basic tracking:

- **What's shown:** The names and values of parameters used in that build.
- **Limitations:** Only the current build's values; there's no historical comparison.

Method 2: Parameterized Trigger Plugin

- **Overview:** A popular Jenkins plugin enhancing parameter handling and tracking.
- **History:** It maintains a history of past builds with the parameters used.
- **Filtering:** You can search and filter past builds based on their parameter choices.
- **Useful for:** Larger projects where tracking parameter trends over time is important.

Example: Deployment Build History (Parameterized Trigger)

1. **Accessing History:** A build has a 'Parameters' section like the core Jenkins feature, but it offers a link like "This build has parameters from other builds". This leads to its detailed history.
2. **What You See**: A table showcasing:
   - The build number where parameter values came from.
   - Each parameter's name and the value used in the current build.
   - A diff view if the parameters differ from those used in the current build.

Method 3: Groovy to the Rescue

For ultimate customization, you can tap into Jenkins' Groovy scripting capabilities within your pipelines.

```
stage('Log Parameters') {
    steps {
        script {
            // Access the parameters
            def buildParams = currentBuild.rawBuild.getAction(ParametersAction.class).getParameters()
            buildParams.each {
                echo "${it.name} = ${it.value}"
            }

            // Potential: Write parameters to a file for external analysis
        }
    }
}
```

Considerations

- **Complexity vs. Insight:** Basic build parameters give you immediate information, plugins provide more in-depth views, while Groovy is for the most tailored tracking.
- **Data Management:** How long do you need to keep parameter history? Some plugins allow you to manage how much data is retained.
- **Integration:** Could you feed parameter data into external monitoring or log analysis tools?

Resources

- **Parameterized Trigger Plugin**
  https://plugins.jenkins.io/parameterized-trigger/

Practice: Design Your Tracking

Think about your most complex parameterized pipelines. Consider:

1. **Audit Trail:** Would you benefit from knowing exactly who triggered builds and the specific parameter choices they made?
2. **Parameter Correlations:** Are there dependencies between certain parameters or common combinations of them that hint at usage patterns?

Let's Strategize! Choose a parameterized pipeline you have. Describe how you would implement either plugin-based parameter tracking or utilize Groovy scripting to enhance your understanding of how it's being used.

Dropdown Selection Parameters Demystified, Part 1

Let's delve into the world of Dropdown Selection Parameters, where users are presented with curated choices to streamline your Jenkins pipelines.

When Choices Need Constraints

String parameters offer flexibility, but sometimes you want these benefits:

- **Error Prevention:** Limit user input to a predefined set to minimize the risk of typos or incorrect values.
- **Discoverability:** Help users easily see what their valid options are.
- **Consistency**: Enforce the use of specific values (e.g., for environment names, version identifiers).

Defining a Dropdown Parameter (Declarative)

```
pipeline {
    parameters {
        choice(name: 'BUILD_TARGET', choices: ['debug', 'release', 'production'], description: 'Select the build target')
    }
    // ... your pipeline stages ...
}
```

Let's break it down:

- **choice:** This tells Jenkins to create a dropdown.
- **name:** The usual parameter name (use `params.BUILD_TARGET`)
- **choices:** A list of the allowed values to populate the dropdown.
- **description:** Helps your users understand the options.

In Action: The User's Perspective

When triggering a build, they'll see a dropdown menu instead of a text box. This helps guide their input.

Example: Selecting Test Scenarios

```
parameters {
    choice(name: 'TEST_SCENARIOS', choices: ['Basic Smoke
Tests', 'Full Regression', 'New Feature Tests'],
description: 'Choose which test scenarios to run')
}
stage('Testing') {
    steps {
        script {
            // Logic here could execute different test
sets based on params.TEST_SCENARIOS
        }
    }
}
```

Beyond the Basics

- **Jenkins Plugins:** Some plugins can extend the 'choice' parameter, allowing you to dynamically fetch the dropdown options from external sources (more on this in Part 2).

Tips and Considerations

- **Choose Wisely:** Dropdown parameters are best when the number of choices is manageable and relatively static.
- **Not for Secrets:** Avoid putting sensitive data into the 'choices' list, as it might be exposed in build logs.
- **Evolving Choices:** If the options need to change frequently, a String parameter coupled with input validation might be a better long-term solution.

Resources

- **Jenkins Documentation (Choice Parameter):**
  https://www.jenkins.io/doc/book/pipeline/syntax/

Practice: Design Your Dropdowns

Think about these situations. Could a dropdown parameter improve the user experience?

- **Deployment Region:** Your application deploys to multiple regions (e.g., 'us-east', 'us-west', 'eu-central').

- **Feature Toggle:** A build parameter to turn a new experimental feature "ON" or "OFF".

Let's Brainstorm! Take one of these scenarios (or your own idea). Describe how you'd implement it with a dropdown parameter, including the exact 'choices' you'd offer.

Dropdown Selection Parameters Demystified, Part 2

Let's continue our exploration of dropdown parameters and how they can add polish and predictability to your Jenkins pipelines!

Dynamic Dropdowns: Powered by Groovy

In Part 1, we focused on static choices defined directly within your Jenkinsfile. Now, let's make those choices dynamic using Jenkins' Groovy scripting capabilities.

Example: Populating from an External File

```
pipeline {
    parameters {
        choice(name: 'SERVER_CONFIG', choices: getServerList(), description: 'Select the target server configuration')
    }
    // ...
}

def getServerList() {
    // Example: Read from a simple text file, one server name per line
    def serverFile = new File('/path/to/server_list.txt')
    return serverFile.readLines()
}
```

- **getServerList()**: A function that uses Groovy to potentially fetch data from anywhere (file, an API call, a database) and returns a list of strings.
- **choices**: The `getServerList()` function now populates the dropdown.

Scenario 2: Active Directory Integration

```
def getDeploymentGroups() {
```

```
    // Logic to query your Active Directory (AD) or LDAP
system
    // for a list of valid deployment groups.
    return ['Production-Admins', 'Staging-Testers',
'Dev-Team']
}
```

Advantages of Dynamic Dropdowns

- **Maintainability:** Update the data source without modifying the `Jenkinsfile` itself.
- **Adaptability:** Reflect changes in your infrastructure or configuration in real-time.
- **Automation:** Can be a part of a larger provisioning or configuration management process.

Security Considerations

- **Input Sanitization (if needed):** If your data source is influenced by users, validate it before injecting it into your parameter choices.
- **Source Reliability:** Ensure the system fetching your dropdown items is secure and trustworthy.

Jenkins Plugins: Expanding Possibilities

Several plugins enhance dropdown parameter functionality:

- **Active Choices Plugin:** Allows dynamic fetching of choices even in Declarative Pipelines. It lets you use a Groovy script to generate choices and even react to other parameter values for cascaded dropdowns!
- **Extended Choice Parameter Plugin:** Introduces new choice types (multi-select, checkbox list, etc.), giving you much more UI flexibility.

Practice: Getting Dynamic

Let's revisit the scenarios from Part 1:

- **Deployment Region:** Could you fetch available regions from your cloud provider's API and populate the dropdown?
- **Feature Toggle:** If feature states were stored in a simple configuration file, could you read them to populate the dropdown?

Troubleshooting Tips

- **Inspect Build Output:** Echo the output of your Groovy functions within your pipeline to see the generated choices.
- **Jenkins Logs:** Check Jenkins system logs for potential plugin errors if your dropdowns behave unexpectedly.

Resources

- **Active Choices Plugin** https://plugins.jenkins.io/uno-choice/
- **Extended Choice Parameter Plugin** https://plugins.jenkins.io/extended-choice-parameter/

Let's Brainstorm! Do you have a scenario where a dynamically populated dropdown would dramatically improve the usability of your parameterized Jenkins pipelines?

Section 8:
Embracing the World of Variables

Variable Exploration: An Introduction

Let's embark on a journey into the realm of variables! These little chameleons hold the power to make your Jenkins pipelines more adaptable and efficient.

Why Variables Matter

Imagine your pipelines are like culinary recipes. Variables act as your ingredients and allow you to:

- **Avoid Hardcoding:** Instead of fixed values, use variables to represent things like build numbers, target environments, configuration settings, file paths, etc. This makes your pipelines reusable.
- **Centralize Information:** Variables act as a single point of reference. If a piece of data needs to change, you might only have to update it in one place rather than searching through your entire pipeline script.
- **External Input:** Variables pave the way for parameters (we've seen those!) and interaction with the Jenkins system itself.

Types of Variables

Let's meet the two main categories in the Jenkins world:

1. **Predefined (Jenkins-Specific)**
    - These are provided automatically by Jenkins.
    - They tell you things like:
        - `BUILD_NUMBER`: The current build number of your job.
        - `JOB_NAME`: The name of the current Jenkins job.
        - `NODE_NAME`: The name of the Jenkins agent executing the build.
        - And many more!
2. **User-Defined**
    - These are variables *you* create within your `Jenkinsfile` or set as parameters.

- They can hold any values you need:
  - Deployment targets: "test", "production"
  - Version numbers: "1.2.5"
  - API Keys (Use with extra caution!)
  - Custom status flags

Using Variables in Your Pipelines

Let's see them in action. This snippet demonstrates both predefined and user-defined variables:

```
pipeline {
    agent any
    stages {
        stage('Prepare Build Info') {
            steps {
                script {
                    // User-defined
                    env.MY_VERSION = '2.0.1'
                }
                echo "Running build #${BUILD_NUMBER} of job ${JOB_NAME}"
                echo "Version set to: ${env.MY_VERSION}"
            }
        }
        // ... other stages using your variable ...
    }
}
```

- **env.** When using variables in Declarative Pipelines, the env. prefix is often needed.
- **${VAR_NAME}** This is how you substitute the value of a variable into your pipeline.

Important Notes

- **Case Sensitivity:** Variables in Jenkins are case-sensitive!
- **Scope:** Where a variable is defined and visible matters (more on this in a later chapter)!

Resources

- **Jenkins Environment Variables**
  https://www.jenkins.io/doc/book/pipeline/jenkinsfile/#environment-variables

Practice Time

1. **Your Pipeline:** Think of a pipeline you already have. List some pieces of information that are currently hardcoded but could be turned into variables.
2. **System Info:** Wouldn't it be useful to have a stage that simply prints out important details about the environment your build is running in? Use Jenkins-specific variables to try this!

Variable Declaration: Defining Your Toolkit

Let's dive into the specifics of how you create your own custom variables within your Jenkins pipelines. Think of this as building your own set of tools to make your processes more adaptable!

Methods of Variable Introduction

There are several ways to bring variables into existence in your pipelines:

Method 1: Simple Assignment (Declarative)

```
pipeline {
    agent any
    stages {
        stage('Example') {
            steps {
                script {
                    env.DEPLOYMENT_MODE = 'staging'
                }
            }
        }
    }
}
```

- **Best for:** Variables with values known in advance.
- **env.:** Remember, in Declarative Pipelines, you usually need the env. prefix to make it available globally.

Method 2: Inside the 'script' Block (Declarative & Scripted)

```
stage('Example') {
   steps {
       script {
           // Scripted Pipeline syntax here...
           def serverName = 'dev-web-01'
           echo "Deploying to server: ${serverName}"
       }
   }
```

}

- **Narrower Scope:** Variables defined *within* a `script` block are generally accessible only within that block.
- **No 'env.' Needed:** The `env.` prefix is not needed when using Scripted Pipeline syntax.

Method 3: The 'environment' Directive (Declarative)

```
environment {
    VERSION_TAG   = 'v1.3.0'
    BUILD_TARGET  = 'production'
}
```

- **Global Impact:** Variables in the `environment` block are accessible throughout all stages of your pipeline.
- **Flexibility:** You can even use other variables or small Groovy expressions within this block.

Key Considerations

- **Naming:** Variable names are case-sensitive. They generally follow standard programming conventions (letters, numbers, underscores, but usually start with a letter).
- **Quotations:** Decide if you need them!
    - 'single quotes': Values are treated literally
    - "double quotes": You can embed other variables inside (e.g., `"Build path: ${env.WORKSPACE}"`)

Example: Setting a Path

```
// This variable is now available in the rest of your pipeline
env.MY_ARTIFACTS_DIR = "${env.WORKSPACE}/build/artifacts"
```

Good Practices

- **Descriptive Names:** Make your variable names self-explanatory.

- **Centralization:** If possible, declare frequently used variables at the top of your `Jenkinsfile` or within an `environment` block for better visibility.

Pro Tip - Dynamic Values with Groovy

Don't underestimate the power of Groovy mixed with variable declaration!

```groovy
// Example:  Get the current date and time
def currentDate = new Date().format('yyyyMMdd-HHmm')
env.BACKUP_FILE_NAME = "database-backup-${currentDate}.sql"
```

Resources

- **Jenkins Pipeline Syntax: Global Variables**
  https://www.jenkins.io/doc/book/pipeline/syntax/#globals

Practice Time

Consider these scenarios. How would you declare variables to represent this information?

1. **File Paths:** You frequently work with files of a specific type. A variable to store a common directory path would be helpful.
2. **API Token:** Your pipeline interacts with an external system using an API key (Remember: handle sensitive data with caution!)

Variable Utilization: Harnessing the Power of Variables

Now that we've learned how to create variables, let's unlock their full potential! In this chapter, we'll see how to truly integrate them into your Jenkins pipelines.

Where Variables Come Into Play

Let's explore the most common places where your variables can make a difference:

1. **Commands Within 'steps'**

   File Paths:

   ```
   sh "cp ${env.SOURCE_CONFIG} ${env.DEPLOYMENT_DIR}"
   ```

   API Endpoints:

   ```
   sh "curl -X POST -d 'status=deployed' ${env.STATUS_TRACKER_URL}"
   ```

2. **Conditional Logic**

   ```
   stage('Deploy To Production?') {
       when {
           environment name: 'DEPLOYMENT_ENV', value: 'production'
       }
       // ... steps to deploy ...
   }
   ```

3. **String Manipulation**

   ```
   def backupFileName = "backup-${env.BUILD_ID}.zip"
   sh "zip ${backupFileName} ${env.ARTIFACTS_TO_BACKUP}"
   ```

4. **Plugin Configuration**
     - Some plugins allow you to reference variables in their settings fields. This varies plugin by plugin.

Key Techniques

- **Substitution:** The fundamental way you use variables – substituting their value into your pipeline logic using `${MyVariable}` syntax.
- **Groovy Expressions:** Variables become even more powerful when mixed with Groovy:

```
env.MAX_RETRIES = env.RETRY_COUNT.toInteger() + 2
```

Utilizing Variables for Dynamic Behavior

Example Scenario: **Customizable Notifications**

```
stage('Notifications') {
    steps {
        script {
            if (env.DEPLOYMENT_TARGET == 'production') {
                // Send alert to a specific channel or distribution list
            } else {
                // Less critical notification
            }
        }
    }
}
```

Cautions & Troubleshooting

- **Scope:** Remember where your variable is defined and visible (we'll discuss this in-depth in a later chapter on Scope).
- **Unset Variables:** If you reference a variable that doesn't exist, your pipeline might error out. Defensive Groovy checks can help.
- **Console Output:** Echo the values of your variables when things aren't behaving as expected to help debug.

Advanced Use Case: Variable-Driven Stages

```
def environments = ['test', 'staging', 'production']

for (env in environments) {
    stage("Deploy to ${env}") {
```

```
        // Deployment steps potentially customized using the 'env' value
    }
}
```

Important Note: Security and Secrets

- **Avoid in Plaintext:** Don't store highly sensitive data (e.g., production API keys) directly in your `Jenkinsfile` for security reasons.
- **Jenkins Credentials:** Jenkins provides a mechanism called "Credentials" specifically designed for secrets management. We'll cover this in a later chapter.

Resources

- **Jenkins Documentation: Using Environment Variables**
  https://www.jenkins.io/doc/book/pipeline/jenkinsfile/#using-environment-variables

Practice: Put Your Variables to Work!

Think about these scenarios:

1. **Test Result Tracking:** Could you store test result counts (passed, failed) in variables and display a summary at the end of your pipeline?
2. **Conditional Cleanup:** Should certain temporary files be deleted only if a build step has succeeded? Variables can help with the decision logic.

Let's Design Improvement!

Choose a pipeline snippet where you're not currently using any variables. Describe the pipeline's functionality. Brainstorm how the introduction of variables could add flexibility or streamline the process.

Navigating Jenkins-Specific Environment Variables, Part 1

Let's embark on a journey exploring the realm of environment variables that Jenkins automatically provides within your pipelines. These are your secret weapons for interacting with the Jenkins environment itself!

The Jenkins Universe at Your Fingertips

Jenkins-specific variables act as windows into the following areas:

- **Build Data:**
    - BUILD_NUMBER: The current build number
    - BUILD_ID: A unique identifier for the current build
    - JOB_NAME: The name of your Jenkins job
    - And more!
- **Node Information:** Where your build is running
    - NODE_NAME: The name of the Jenkins agent executing the build
    - NODE_LABELS: Labels associated with the agent
- **Workspace:**
    - WORKSPACE: The absolute path of the workspace directory on the agent where your build is running

Why These Matter

1. **Informative Actions:**
    - Embed the build number in artifacts or log files for traceability
    - Customize notifications or reports based on whether it's a production or development environment build.
2. **Conditional Behavior:**
    - Execute a cleanup task only if the build runs on a specific type of agent.
3. **Troubleshooting:**
    - Echo node and workspace information to help debug issues related to your build environment.

Common Use Cases

- **Timestamping Artifacts:**

```
env.ARCHIVE_NAME = "application-${env.BUILD_ID}.zip"
```

- **Branch-Aware Logic:**

```
if (env.BRANCH_NAME == 'main') {
    // Special steps for the main branch
}
```

- **Workspace Paths:**

```
sh "ls -la ${env.WORKSPACE}"
```

Discovering Available Variables

There are two main ways to find the full treasure chest of variables:

1. **Jenkins UI:**
   - From your job's page, click "Environment Variables" in the sidebar. This is a good quick reference.
2. **In Your Pipeline:** For a more dynamic view, try a stage like this:

```
stage('Inspect Environment') {
    steps {
        sh 'printenv' // Linux/MacOS
        sh 'set' // Windows
    }
}
```

Part 1 Focus: Build-Related Variables

Let's look at some common build-related variables and how they might be used:

Variable	Description	Example Usage
BUILD_NUMBER	The sequential number of the current build for the job	Tagging Docker images like

		myapp:build-${BUI LD_NUMBER}
JOB_NAME	The name of the Jenkins job	Custom email subject: "[{JOB_NAME}]: Build #{BUILD_NUMBER} Status"
BUILD_URL	The URL to access the current build's page	Sending a Slack notification with a link to the build log
JOB_BASE_NAME	The job name without any parameters. Useful for scenarios with parameterized jobs	Creating custom folder names that remain consistent even with parameters

Resources

- Jenkins Wiki: Environment Variables
  https://plugins.jenkins.io/pipeline-model-definition/ (See the "Environment Variables" section)

Practice Time

1. **Artifact Naming:** How could you incorporate the JOB_NAME and BUILD_NUMBER into the naming of the zip files your pipeline generates?
2. **Debugging Aid:** Imagine you are sometimes facing issues that seem specific to certain build agents. How could a stage using Jenkins-specific variables help pinpoint the problem?

Navigating Jenkins-Specific Environment Variables, Part 2

Let's continue our exploration of Jenkins-specific environment variables! In Part 2, we'll focus on those that reveal details about your build environment and how to make the most of them.

Agents and Workspaces: The Backbone of Your Builds

- **NODE_NAME:** Crucial for knowing *which* agent your build is running on. This might be a machine's hostname or a label you've assigned.
- **NODE_LABELS:** Agents can have labels (e.g., 'linux', 'windows-gpu-build'). This variable gives you access to these labels.
- **WORKSPACE:** The absolute path to your build's working directory on the agent. Indispensable when working with files.

Use Cases

1. **Resource-Aware Logic**

```
node('linux') { // Ensure you're on a Linux agent
    stage('Build') {
        // ... Steps for compiling a Linux binary ...
    }
}
```

2. **Conditional Post-Build Actions**

```
stage('Archive') {
    when {
        expression { env.NODE_NAME == 'archiving-server-01' }
    }
    steps {
```

```
            // Copy artifacts to a long-term storage
location
        }
}
```

3. **Building File Paths**

   ```
   sh "cp ${env.WORKSPACE}/target/my-application.jar
   ${env.WORKSPACE}/releases/"
   ```

Pro Tips

- **Pipeline vs. Node:** Remember, some variables relate to the overall pipeline (like JOB_NAME), while others are specific to the node/agent where a stage is executing.
- **Dynamic Paths:** Constructing paths by combining WORKSPACE with other variables provides flexibility and resilience to changes in your Jenkins setup.

Workspace Cleanup

A common pattern using the WORKSPACE variable is for tailored workspace cleanup:

```
stage('Cleanup') {
    steps {
        deleteDir() // Jenkins 'deleteDir' step for cleanup works with WORKSPACE
    }
}
```

A Note on Declarative vs. Scripted

In Declarative Pipelines, accessing Jenkins-specific environment variables often requires using the sh or bat steps to execute small scripts where you can then reference them.

Example: Declarative with a Script Snippet

```
stage('Environment Info') {
    steps {
```

```
        sh 'echo "Running on node: $NODE_NAME"'
    }
}
```

Resources

- **Jenkins Documentation** lists a broader set of even more niche Jenkins-specific variables: https://www.jenkins.io/doc/

Practice

1. **Multi-OS Builds:** Could you design a pipeline where build steps are routed to different agent types (Windows, Linux, etc.) based on the NODE_LABELS variable?
2. **Efficient Cleanup:** You have a pipeline that produces large temporary files. Devise a strategy using WORKSPACE and potentially node labels to clean up only these files under the right conditions.

Let's Troubleshoot!

Imagine a scenario where your builds sometimes behave differently depending on the build agent. Describe how Jenkins-specific environment variables could assist you in pinpointing the root cause of this variance.

Section 9: Mastering Advanced Jenkins Techniques

Building a Healthy Pipeline: Understanding Build Health

Let's dive into the concept of build health in Jenkins, a cornerstone in maintaining reliable and efficient CI/CD processes.

Why Build Health Matters

A "healthy" build in the Jenkins world goes beyond just a green "success" indicator. It implies:

- **Trustworthiness:** Your pipeline consistently produces the expected outcomes.
- **Early Issue Detection:** Problems are surfaced quickly, preventing them from cascading into larger failures.
- **Actionable Insights:** Jenkins provides the data you need to pinpoint and rectify the root causes of failures.
- **Maintainability:** Your pipelines are designed to be resilient and easy to troubleshoot.

The Anatomy of Build Health

Let's break down the elements that contribute to a healthy Jenkins pipeline:

1. **Test Results**

- **Unit Tests:** Do your low-level code components function as intended?
- **Integration Tests:** Do various parts of your system work together correctly?
- **Code Coverage:** What percentage of your code is actually exercised by your tests?
- **Trends:** Are test results improving over time, or are new issues creeping in?

2. **Static Code Analysis**
   - **Quality Metrics:** Is your code maintainable, well-structured, free of potential bugs, and adhering to coding standards?
   - **Linting:** Catches stylistic issues and common programming errors (tools like SonarQube, ESLint, etc.)
3. **Build Stability**
   - **Failure Rates:** How often do builds fail, and why?
   - **Intermittent Issues:** Beware of those flaky tests or sporadic build hiccups!
4. **Artifacts**
   - **Expected Output:** Are the build processes creating the correct deliverables (binaries, packages, etc.)?
   - **Artifact Management:** Are these artifacts stored and versioned properly?

Key Features in Jenkins

Jenkins offers a suite of tools to monitor and analyze build health:

- **Build Status:** The most basic indicator - Success, Unstable, Failed, etc.
- **Console Output:** Provides detailed logs for diagnosis.
- **Test Result Reporting:** Jenkins integrates with testing frameworks (JUnit, etc.) to visualize test trends.
- **Plugins:** Plugins extend Jenkins with warnings for static code analysis issues, code coverage reports, and more.

Proactive Strategies

1. **Define "Healthy":** What are the acceptable thresholds for test pass rates, code quality metrics, allowable build failure rates, etc.?
2. **Fail Fast:** Configure your pipelines to halt if critical steps or tests fail.
3. **Notifications:** Set up alerts to quickly notify your team of build health issues.

4. **Review and Refactor:** Use the insights Jenkins gives you to iteratively improve your code, tests, and your pipeline logic itself.

"Unstable" Builds

Jenkins offers the concept of 'unstable' builds. This is a useful middle ground:

- **Indicates Issues:** Something is wrong, even if the pipeline didn't outright fail.
- **Allows Downstream Flow:** Subsequent stages or dependent jobs might continue.
- **Triggers Attention:** Useful for things like test pass rates dropping below a desired level.

Example: Pipeline Health Dashboard

```
stage('Health Dashboard') {
    steps {
        junit '**/target/surefire-reports/*.xml'   //
Collect test results
        step([$class: 'WarningsPublisher',
            healthy: 100,
            unHealthy: 0,
            consoleParsers: [$class:
'AntAdvancedWarningsParser']
        ]) // Example of a plugin-based static analysis
integration
    }
}
```

Resources

- **Jenkins JUnit Plugin:** https://plugins.jenkins.io/junit/
- **Jenkins Warnings Next Generation Plugin:** https://plugins.jenkins.io/warnings-ng/

Practice

Consider your current Jenkins pipelines.

1. **Metrics:** What build health metrics are you already tracking, if any?

2. **Gaps:** Are there areas (code quality, test coverage, etc.) where you'd like greater visibility?

Describe a real-world scenario where a specific build health issue caused problems for your team (e.g., flaky test, intermittent network errors). Brainstorm how Jenkins could have been used to expose and mitigate the issue proactively.

Unraveling Issues: Advanced Troubleshooting Techniques

When things go wrong, being able to efficiently diagnose the problem is a superpower for any DevOps professional.

Beyond the Basics

While understanding Jenkins' build status and console output is fundamental, complex scenarios demand a deeper dive. This chapter will arm you with the mindset and strategies to tackle those stickiest of pipeline problems.

The Troubleshooting Mindset

- **Reproduce the Issue:** Can you reliably make the failure happen? Intermittent problems are the most difficult to solve.
- **Isolate the Problem:** Break down your pipeline into stages. Which stage is the culprit?
- **Hypothesize and Test:** Think about potential causes (recent code changes, plugin updates, etc.), and devise ways to test your theories.
- **Version Control is Your Friend:** Can you compare changes in your pipeline code or Jenkins configuration that might correlate with when the issue began?

Key Areas to Investigate

1. **Jenkins Environment**
    - **Logs:** Jenkins logs (found under Manage Jenkins -> System Log) might reveal issues with Jenkins itself.
    - **Resource Exhaustion:** Is your Jenkins server running out of disk space, memory, or CPU? (Monitoring tools are helpful here!)
    - **Plugin Conflicts:** Did you recently update any plugins? Check for known plugin incompatibilities or bugs.

2. **Pipeline Logic**
   - **Groovy Errors:** If using Scripted Pipeline, is a syntax error creeping in? Echo variables for debugging.
   - **Assumptions:** Are you depending on a file existing, a network resource being available, etc.? Build in safeguards!
   - **Step Configuration:** Review any plugin-specific steps – wrong parameters can lead to unexpected behavior.
3. **External Dependencies**
   - **Network:** Can your build reach other systems it needs (artifact repositories, external APIs)?
   - **Credentials:** Are the credentials used in your pipeline valid and have the necessary permissions?
   - **Changes Upstream:** Did some other system you rely on change its API or behavior?

Advanced Techniques

1. **Verbose Output:** Many Jenkins plugins and even the 'sh' command support a 'verbose' mode for extra logging detail.
2. **Declarative Debugging:** Declarative Pipelines can use the 'input' step to pause a build and allow you to inject modified values to test hypotheses.
3. **Remote Debugging (Scripted)**: It's possible to connect a debugger to a Scripted Jenkins Pipeline! (This is a very advanced technique).
4. **Replay Feature:** Some Jenkins plugins offer the ability to re-run pipelines or individual stages, aiding in diagnosis.

Example: The Case of the Disappearing Artifact

Scenario: Your deployment stage fails because a file generated by the build stage is missing! Let's troubleshoot:

- **Check Workspace:** Is the file actually being produced during the build?
- **Examine File Paths:** Are the build and deployment stages working with the correct paths to the artifact?
- **Cleanup Logic:** Did a cleanup step mistakenly delete your artifact?
- **Permissions:** Does the Jenkins agent process have the appropriate permissions to create and read the artifact?

Resources

- **Jenkins Pipeline: Debugging**
  https://www.jenkins.io/doc/book/pipeline/jenkinsfile/#debugging

Practice

Think of a past tricky Jenkins issue you resolved.

- **The Problem:** Briefly describe the issue.
- **Your Approach:** How did you approach troubleshooting it?
- **The 'Aha' Moment:** What tipped you off to the root cause?

Safeguarding Secrets: Managing Credentials in Jenkins

Let's embark on a mission to protect your most sensitive information within the world of Jenkins! Improper secrets management can have disastrous consequences, so this chapter is essential.

What are Secrets?

In the Jenkins context, secrets encompass:

- **Passwords:** For databases, external systems, or user accounts
- **API Tokens:** Used to authenticate with services
- **SSH Keys:** Granting access to code repositories or remote servers
- **Certificates:** SSL/TLS certificates for secure communication

The Risks of Mishandling Secrets

1. **Hardcoding in Jenkinsfiles:**
   - Secrets become visible in your version control history.
   - Compromises any environment where the `Jenkinsfile` is used.
2. **Plaintext in the Environment:**
   - Exposes secrets to anyone or any process that can see the Jenkins environment (logs, troubleshooting dumps, etc.).

Jenkins to the Rescue: The Credentials System

Jenkins has a built-in subsystem specifically designed to securely store and manage secrets:

- **Centralization:** Instead of being scattered around, secrets live in one place.
- **Scope:** Control which pipelines/jobs can access which secrets.
- **Types:** Jenkins supports a variety of secret types out of the box.
- **Plugins:** The Credentials system is extensible with plugins.

Kinds of Credentials

- **Secret Text:** Simple strings like passwords or tokens
- **Username with Password:** Classic combo
- **Secret File:** Useful for things like private keys
- **SSH Username with private key**
- **Certificates**
- **Docker registry credentials**
- **And more** depending on plugins installed

Using Credentials in Your Pipelines

Let's see how to reference stored credentials:

Example: Declarative Pipeline

```
pipeline {

    agent any

    stages {

        stage('Deploy') {

            environment {

                // Assuming credentials with ID 'production-database' exist

                DB_PASSWORD = credentials('production-database')

            }

            steps {

                sh "mysql -u appuser -p${DB_PASSWORD} ..."

            }
```

            }
        }
}

Example: Scripted Pipeline

```
stage('Deploy') {
    steps {
        withCredentials([usernamePassword(credentialsId: 'production-database',
                                          usernameVariable: 'DB_USER',
                                          passwordVariable: 'DB_PASSWORD')]) {
            sh "mysql -u ${DB_USER} -p${DB_PASSWORD} ..."
        }
    }
}
```

Best Practices

- **No in Plaintext:** Avoid putting secrets directly in your pipeline code. Always use the credentials mechanisms.
- **Principle of Least Privilege:** Grant only the minimum access necessary to your pipelines.
- **Audit and Rotate:** Regularly review your stored credentials and change any compromised or leaked secrets.

Resources

- **Jenkins Documentation: Using Credentials**
  https://www.jenkins.io/doc/book/using/using-credentials/

Practice: Examine Your Secrets

Think about your current Jenkins pipelines…

1. **Are Sensitive Values Exposed?** Do you have any hardcoded passwords, tokens, or keys that should be moved into Credentials?
2. **Scope Audit:** Could you tighten the access control on any of your existing credentials?

Decoding Jenkinsfile Naming Conventions

Let's embark on a journey to understand the hidden patterns and best practices within the world of Jenkinsfile naming. While these might seem like minor details, proper naming conventions bring clarity and maintainability to your Jenkins setup!

Why Naming Matters

1. **Discoverability:** Especially in large projects or teams, being able to quickly find the right Jenkinsfile is essential.
2. **Organization:** Names can reflect project structure, pipeline type, or even the environments they target.
3. **Self-Documentation:** A well-named Jenkinsfile gives a hint about its purpose without even needing to open it.
4. **Version Control Friendliness:** Good names play nicely with how branches work in your source control system.

Common Naming Approaches

There are no absolute rules, but here are several widely used patterns:

- **Jenkinsfile (Simple & Direct):** Works best when you have a single pipeline per project.
- **Jenkinsfile.<branch_name> :** Useful for Multibranch Pipelines where behavior might differ across branches (e.g., `Jenkinsfile.main`, `Jenkinsfile.develop`).

- **Jenkinsfile.<purpose>** : Highlights the type of pipeline (e.g., `Jenkinsfile.build`, `Jenkinsfile.test`, `Jenkinsfile.deploy`).
- **<project-name>_Jenkinsfile:** Helpful when you have multiple related projects in a repository and need to distinguish their pipelines.

Best Practices

- **Consistency:** Pick a convention and stick to it within your team or organization.
- **Clarity over Brevity:** A slightly longer but clearer name is usually better.
- **Avoid Special Characters:** Spaces and most punctuation can create issues with some tools. Stick to letters, numbers, hyphens, and underscores.
- **Balance Specificity:** Encode enough information to be useful, but avoid overly long, complex names.

Real-World Examples

Scenario	Possible Jenkinsfile Naming
A single pipeline for a project named 'webapp'	`Jenkinsfile`
Separate build and deploy pipelines for 'webapp'	`Jenkinsfile.build` `Jenkinsfile.deploy`
Multibranch pipeline for 'webapp', main branch	`Jenkinsfile` `Jenkinsfile.feature-X`
Multiple microservices within one repository	`order-service_Jenkinsfile` `inventory-service_Jenkinsfile`

Special Case: Declarative vs. Scripted

While naming conventions apply to both, Declarative Pipelines often favor a single, more generic `Jenkinsfile`. This is because their structure is more rigid, so the filename itself is less descriptive of the actual pipeline logic.

Example: When Specificity Helps

Imagine you have pipelines for both production and staging deployments. Consider:

- `Jenkinsfile.deploy` - Ambiguous. Where does it deploy?
- `Jenkinsfile.deploy-production` - Immediately clear!

Pro Tip: Version Control to the Rescue

If you need more metadata than the filename allows, consider a small text file *alongside* your `Jenkinsfile` (e.g., `README.txt` or similar) with additional details – purpose, owner, last-modified date, etc.

Resources

While there's no definitive standard, you might find inspiration in these:

- **Jenkins GitHub Org:** Many official Jenkins-related projects have their Jenkinsfiles publicly visible https://github.com/jenkins-infra

Practice: Audit Your Pipelines

1. **Take Inventory:** Do you currently have a consistent naming scheme? If not, what inconsistencies exist?
2. **Room for Improvement:** Could any of your Jenkinsfiles benefit from a more descriptive name?

Let's Refine!

Describe a real-world Jenkins project you've worked on (or a hypothetical one). Let's brainstorm potential Jenkinsfile naming strategies that would be a good fit for its structure and the way your team works.

Juggling Jenkinsfiles: Managing Multiple Jenkinsfiles

Let's dive into the scenarios where having multiple Jenkinsfiles becomes a powerful tool in your Jenkins arsenal and how to manage them effectively.

Why Go Beyond a Single Jenkinsfile?

1. **Complex Projects:**
   - Different pipelines for build, test, deployment, etc., might warrant separate definitions.
   - Large monorepos might contain sub-projects that each need their own pipeline.
2. **Multibranch Pipelines:** Individual Jenkinsfiles tailor behavior per branch.
3. **Separation of Concerns:** Decoupling frequently changing pipeline logic from more stable Jenkins setup can improve maintainability.
4. **Reusability:** Common pipeline logic can be put in shared Jenkinsfiles and included in others.

When to Keep It Simple

- **Small Projects:** A single Jenkinsfile might suffice for straightforward CI/CD.
- **Infrequent Changes:** If your pipeline is stable, the overhead of multiple files might be unnecessary.

Common Patterns

Let's look at typical ways to organize multiple Jenkinsfiles:

- **Side-by-Side** (at the root of your repository)
    - `Jenkinsfile.build`
    - `Jenkinsfile.deploy-staging`
    - `Jenkinsfile.deploy-prod`
- **Subdirectories**
    - `backend/Jenkinsfile`
    - `frontend/Jenkinsfile`
    - This aligns nicely with project structure.
- **Hybrid**
    - A main `Jenkinsfile` for generic steps
    - Specialized Jenkinsfiles in subdirectories for project-specific logic

Techniques for Managing Complexity

1. **Shared Libraries:** Jenkins has a mechanism for creating reusable pipeline code. (We'll cover this in a later chapter!)
2. **Templating:** Tools like Jinja2 or simple scripting can help generate Jenkinsfiles from templates to reduce repetition.
3. **Configuration as Code (CasC):** The 'Jenkins Configuration as Code' plugin lets you manage certain aspects of Jenkins setup declaratively. This can play a role in how you handle multiple Jenkinsfiles.

Example: Microservice Architecture

Imagine you have several microservices in a monorepo. A structure like this is sensible:

```
Jenkinsfile  (Top-level basic pipeline)
services/
   order-service/
      Jenkinsfile
   inventory-service/
      Jenkinsfile
   customer-service/
      Jenkinsfile
```

Controlling Which Jenkinsfile Is Used

- **Declarative:** The pipeline syntax itself has options for specifying which Jenkinsfile to load.
- **Multibranch:** The configuration of the Multibranch Pipeline determines Jenkinsfile discovery.
- **UI/Manual:** When creating a Jenkins job, you can often explicitly input the path to your Jenkinsfile.

Pro Tip: Versioning Your Pipelines

Treat your Jenkinsfiles as code! Source control (Git, etc.) is essential for:

- Tracking changes over time
- Rollback in case new pipeline logic introduces problems
- Collaboration if multiple people work on your pipelines

Resources

- **Jenkins Shared Libraries**
  https://www.jenkins.io/doc/book/pipeline/shared-libraries/

Practice

Consider your current or past Jenkins projects:

1. **Are Multiple Jenkinsfiles Needed?** Are there areas of your CI/CD where splitting things up could lead to better organization or modularity?
2. **Structure:** If you were to adopt multiple Jenkinsfiles, sketch out how you would organize them within your project's repository.

Putting Theory into Practice: Demystifying Multiple Jenkinsfiles with a Live Demo

Let's turn those multiple Jenkinsfile concepts into reality. In this chapter, we'll work through a hands-on demo showcasing the power and flexibility this technique offers.

Prerequisites

- A running Jenkins instance.
- Basic familiarity with creating Jenkins jobs and pipeline syntax.
- A local code repository (we'll use Git) with a sample project to experiment on.

Our Demo Scenario

We'll simulate a simplified microservice-like architecture. Imagine our project has these components:

- **Backend Service (Node.js):** Handles core business logic
- **Frontend Web App (React):** The user interface
- **Database Setup (Scripts):** Provisions a test database

Goals

- Create separate Jenkinsfiles for each component's build/test process.

- Set up a top-level Jenkinsfile to orchestrate the overall flow.

Step-by-Step Guide

1. **Project Structure**

```
project-root/
    Jenkinsfile         # Top-level pipeline
    backend/
        Jenkinsfile     # Backend-specific logic
        package.json
        ... (backend code)
    frontend/
        Jenkinsfile     # Frontend-specific logic
        package.json
        ... (frontend code)
    database/
        Jenkinsfile     # DB setup logic
        setup.sql
        ...
```

2. **Jenkinsfiles (Simplified)**

project-root/Jenkinsfile

```
pipeline {
    agent any
    stages {
        stage('Build Backend') {
            steps { dir('backend') { script { sh 'npm install' } } }
        }
        stage('Build Frontend') {
            steps { dir('frontend') { script { sh 'npm install' } } }
        }
        // ... add testing, deployment as needed
    }
}
```

backend/Jenkinsfile

```
pipeline {
    agent { label 'nodejs' }
    stages {
        stage('Test') {
            steps { sh 'npm test' }
        }
    }
}
```

(frontend/Jenkinsfile and database/Jenkinsfile – Similar Idea)

3. **Jenkins Setup**
    - **Method 1: Multibranch Pipeline**
        - Great for Git integration – discovers Jenkinsfiles in branches.
    - **Method 2: Manual Job Creation**
        - Create separate Jenkins jobs, pointing each to the relevant Jenkinsfile.

Demo Execution

- Trigger the top-level build (either via Multibranch auto-discovery or manually).
- Observe Jenkins running stages from the main Jenkinsfile, which in turn execute stages within the specialized Jenkinsfiles.

Key Takeaways

- **Modularity:** Changes to the backend don't require modifying the frontend pipeline and vice-versa.
- **Agent Specialization:** The backend Jenkinsfile used a 'nodejs' agent, tailoring the environment.
- **Potential for Reuse:** Imagine packaging common logic into shared libraries used across your Jenkinsfiles.

Extending the Demo

- **Parameterization:** Pass versions, config data from the top level down.
- **Conditional Execution:** when directives to skip parts based on conditions.

- **Deployment:** Add deployment pipelines in separate Jenkinsfiles triggered at the end of your main flow.

Let's Brainstorm!

Do you have a specific project structure in mind where you're considering multiple Jenkinsfiles? Describe the components involved and brainstorm the best way to break down your CI/CD process into pipelines!

Debugging Secrets: Advanced Techniques for Troubleshooting

Secrets-related problems within pipelines can be notoriously tricky to diagnose. Let's arm you with the tools and mindsets needed to tackle them.

The Challenge with Secrets

- **Invisibility:** Unlike regular build failures, the contents of secrets are intentionally hidden in logs and output for security reasons.
- **Access Permissions:** You might not have direct access to the Jenkins Credentials store to verify a secret or its contents.
- **External Dependencies:** Secrets often represent access tokens to other systems. Issues might lie outside Jenkins itself.

Common Scenarios

Let's outline typical situations where secrets-related failures crop up:

1. **Incorrect Value:** A typo in the credential ID, the secret was mistyped, or it was changed on the external system's side.
2. **Insufficient Scopes:** The credentials you're using are valid but lack the necessary permissions (e.g., read-only when you need write access).
3. **Network/Connectivity:** Jenkins can't reach the external system the secret authenticates against.

4. **Expiration/Rotation:** Some secrets are time-limited. Has yours expired?

Advanced Debugging Strategies

1. **Start Simple: Isolate the Issue**
   - **Credentials Testing:** If possible, are you able to use the secret successfully *outside* of Jenkins (e.g., a CLI tool)? This helps determine if the issue is Jenkins-specific.
   - **Hardcoding (Temporarily!):** Can you temporarily replace the secret with a known-good plaintext value in your pipeline for testing? If this works, the problem is likely with the credential itself.
2. **Verbose Output (When Possible)**
   - Many plugins and the 'sh' step support verbose modes that might reveal more clues without exposing the secret's value (e.g., HTTP error codes from an API call).
3. **"Synthetic" Secrets**
   - Create a dummy credential with minimal permissions. Does your pipeline behave differently, giving a hint about the required access level?
4. **Audit Trails**
   - Depending on your external systems, they might log authentication attempts (successful or failed). This can correlate with your Jenkins builds.
5. **Divide and Conquer**
   - Simplify your pipeline to the bare minimum needed to reproduce the error. This reduces the number of moving parts.

Proactive Measures

- **Test Secrets Early:** Have a pipeline stage purely designed to test if a set of secrets can be retrieved and used to perform a basic, safe operation.
- **Secret Rotation Practices:** If your systems support it, rotate secrets regularly. This helps uncover Jenkins pipelines that might unknowingly be using stale credentials.

Example: The Case of the Failed Artifact Deployment

- **Symptom:** Your deployment stage fails with "Authentication Error" when trying to push an artifact to a private repository.

- **Troubleshooting Steps**
    1. **Check Connectivity:** Can Jenkins server reach the artifact repository at all?
    2. **Test the Credentials:** Use a tool like `curl` with the credentials outside of Jenkins to perform a simple listing operation on the repo.
    3. **Examine Permissions:** Does the secret have write access to the repository?
    4. **Consider Timing:** Did the credential recently expire?

Practice

Think back to a past issue you had in Jenkins where a secret might have been the culprit (even if you didn't realize it at the time).

- **The Problem** (briefly)
- **How You Solved It**
- **Knowing What You Know Now** – Could any of the techniques in this chapter have sped up the diagnosis?

Brainstorm Challenge

Describe a hypothetical *but realistic* failure scenario in your Jenkins pipelines that could be caused by an issue with secrets. Brainstorm troubleshooting steps and what clues to look for.

Conditional Logic Unleashed, Part 1: Mastering If Statements

Let's empower you to craft pipelines that intelligently branch and adapt their behavior using the power of 'if' statements.

Why Conditional Logic Matters

1. **Customization:** Not every build needs the exact same steps. React to build parameters, branch names, test results, etc.
2. **Targeted Actions:** Deploy only if certain conditions are met; send notifications based on outcomes.
3. **Efficiency:** Avoid running unnecessary stages, saving time and resources.
4. **Resilience:** Handle potential errors or external factors gracefully within your pipeline's flow.

The 'if' in Jenkins

Jenkins pipelines offer several ways to introduce conditional logic. We'll focus on the most essential building blocks:

- **'when' Directive:** Controls whether an entire stage or step should execute based on various criteria.
- **Groovy Expressions:** Inside 'if' conditions in Scripted Pipelines, you have the flexibility of the Groovy language.

Common 'when' Conditions

- **branch'** : Execute differently based on the branch being built (Multibranch Pipelines)
- **environment'**: Check the value of environment variables.
- **expression** : Any valid Groovy expression (provides the most flexibility)
- **changeset**: Check for changes in specific files or patterns.
- **And more...** explore your Jenkins installation's available 'when' conditions!

Example: Test Results and Deployment

```
stage('Deploy to Production') {
    when {
        expression { return currentBuild.result == 'SUCCESS' }
    }
    steps {
        // Deployment steps here
    }
}
```

Nesting and Combining Conditions

- **Logical Operators:** Use '&&' (and), '||' (or), and '!' (not) within your 'when' expressions or Groovy 'if' blocks.
- **Nesting Stages:** For complex logic, nest stages with their own 'when' conditions.

Groovy Power-Ups (Scripted Pipelines)

- **Variables:**

```
def isReleaseBuild =
currentBuild.displayName.contains("release")
stage('Special Release Tasks') {
    when { isReleaseBuild }
    // ...
}
```

- **External Data:**

```
stage ('Check Feature Toggle') {
    when {
```

```
        expression {
            sh "curl -s
http://feature-toggle-service/featureX" == "enabled"
        }
    }
    // ...
}
```

Best Practices

- **Readability Counts:** Use clear variable names and comments, especially for complex conditions.
- **Start Simple, Iterate:** Begin with small conditional blocks and expand your logic as needed.
- **Test Thoroughly:** Ensure all branches of your conditional logic behave as expected with various inputs.

Pro-Tip: Visual Pipeline Tools

Some Jenkins plugins offer visualization of your pipeline structure, making it easier to grasp conditional flows (e.g., Blue Ocean plugin)

Resources

- **Jenkins Pipeline Documentation: 'when' directive**
  https://www.jenkins.io/doc/book/pipeline/syntax/#when

Practice

Consider the following:

- **Existing Pipeline:** Do you have a pipeline where adding an 'if' statement could improve its behavior?
- **Conditional Challenge:** Describe a real-world scenario where you'd want to execute certain Jenkins actions only if specific criteria are met.

Conditional Logic Unleashed, Part 2: Advanced If Statements Techniques

Going Beyond the Basics

In Part 1, we laid the foundation for 'if' statements and the 'when' directive. Now, let's explore techniques that will enhance your pipeline's decision-making finesse.

Jenkins Functions Within Conditions

Several built-in pipeline functions provide information you can use within your conditions:

- **fileExists:** Check if a file exists in your workspace.
- **changelogContains:** Inspect your commit messages for certain patterns
- **currentBuild.result:** React to the outcome of previous stages (e.g., "SUCCESS" or "FAILURE").
- **params:** Access parameters in parameterized pipelines.

Example: Build Only if Configuration Changed

```
stage('Build (If Changed)') {
    when {
        changeset glob: 'config/**/*'
    }
    steps {
        // Build logic here
    }
}
```

Complex Groovy Expressions

Remember, when using 'expression' conditions or Groovy 'if' blocks, you wield the full power of the Groovy language:

- **String Manipulation:** Search for substrings, use regular expressions, etc.
- **API Calls:** `sh "curl -s https://api.example.com/status" == "OK"` (Query external systems).
- **Advanced Logic:** Utilize Groovy's control flow structures within your conditions.

Predefined Global Variables

Jenkins offers some useful global variables available to your pipelines:

- **env.BRANCH_NAME** : In multibranch pipelines, tells you the branch being built.
- **env.CHANGE_ID** : Identifies the changeset triggering the build (if relevant).

Tip: Explore Available Globals

In your Jenkins instance, navigate to "Manage Jenkins" -> "Script Console". This allows you to experiment and discover the global variables at your disposal.

Example: Deploy from Main Branch with Manual Approval

```
stage('Approve Deployment') {
    when { branch 'main' }
    steps {
        input message: 'Deploy to Production?'
```

```
            // ... (Deployment steps if approved)
        }
}
```

Cascading Decisions with Nested 'if'

For multi-layered logic, nesting 'if' statements (Scripted Pipelines) or 'when' conditions within stages is your superpower:

```
stage('Analysis') {
    when {
        expression {
env.JOB_NAME.contains("DataProcessing") }
    }
    steps {
        script {
            if (env.BUILD_NUMBER.toInteger() % 2 == 0) {
                // Run extra analysis steps
            }
        }
    }
}
```

Best Practices

- **Function Creation:** For complex logic, encapsulate it into reusable Jenkins Shared Library functions.
- **Testing Rigor:** Add dedicated testing stages when your conditional logic gets sophisticated.
- **Judicious Use:** Overly complex branching can make pipelines hard to understand. Strike a balance!

Resources

- **Jenkins Pipeline Steps Reference**
  https://www.jenkins.io/doc/pipeline/steps/ (Search for specific steps like 'fileExists')

Practice

Think about these scenarios:

1. **Selective Notifications:** How would you send a failure notification *only* if it's a production-related job, and the previous build succeeded?
2. **Dynamic Downstream Triggers:** Could you trigger different downstream pipelines based on the contents of a file changed in the current build?

Function Fundamentals, Part 1: Exploring Functionality in Jenkins

Let's embark on a journey into the realm of functions within Jenkins pipelines! We'll empower you to streamline your pipelines, making them more modular and reusable.

Why Functions Matter

1. **Reduce Repetition (DRY):** Write logic once, use it in multiple places. Enforce the "Don't Repeat Yourself" principle.
2. **Organization:** Break down complex pipelines into digestible, well-named functions.
3. **Abstraction:** Hide implementation details behind functions, making your pipelines more readable.
4. **Testability:** Functions can be tested independently, improving pipeline reliability.

Types of Functions in Jenkins

There are two primary ways to introduce functions into your pipelines:

1. **Scripted Pipelines: Groovy Power**

- Define functions directly within your `Jenkinsfile` using Groovy syntax (`def`).
- Maximum flexibility, as you can leverage all of Groovy's language features.
2. **Jenkins Shared Libraries**
    - Functions defined in separate `.groovy` files, intended for sharing across pipelines.
    - Promote better organization and reuse, especially in larger teams or projects.
    - We'll cover Shared Libraries in a later chapter.

Scripted Pipeline Function Basics

```
def deployToStaging() {
    // Deployment logic for the staging environment here
    sh "deploy-script --env staging"
}

stage('Deploy') {
    deployToStaging()
}
```

Key Points

- **Parameters:** Functions can take parameters to customize their behavior.
- **Return Values:** Functions can return values to be used in other parts of your pipeline.
- **Global vs. Local:** Be mindful of whether you define the function globally in your `Jenkinsfile` or within a specific node/stage block.

Example: Parameterized Build Step

```
def runBuild(language, buildTool) {
    if (language == 'java') {
        sh "${buildTool} build"
    } else if (language == 'python') {
        sh "${buildTool} setup.py build"
    }
```

```
    // ... add more languages as needed
}

stage('Build') {
    runBuild('java', 'mvn')
}
```

Common Use Cases for Functions

- **Complex Deployment Logic:** Encapsulate deployment steps that differ across environments.
- **Notifications:** Create functions like sendSuccessNotification or sendFailureNotification.
- **External Interactions:** Interact with REST APIs or other systems.
- **Custom Build/Test Steps:** Package up a sequence of shell commands or tool invocations.

Best Practices

- **Meaningful Names:** Your function names should clearly describe their purpose.
- **Small and Focused:** Each function should ideally do one thing well.
- **Comments:** Add comments to explain non-obvious logic, especially for complex functions.

Pro Tip: The 'Global Pipeline Library'

Jenkins lets you manage frequently used functions in one place. Navigate to "Manage Jenkins" -> "Global Pipeline Libraries" for this feature.

Resources

- **Jenkins Documentation: Defining Functions**
  https://www.jenkins.io/doc/book/pipeline/shared-libraries/#defining-functions

Practice

Consider your current Jenkins pipelines…

1. **Repetitive Blocks:** Are there chunks of steps you copy-paste frequently? These could be candidates for turning into functions.

2. **Abstraction Opportunity:** Are some parts of your pipeline hard to understand at a glance? Could a well-named function make them clearer?

Let's Build Functions!

Describe a common task in your Jenkins pipelines that involves several steps. Brainstorm how to refactor it into a reusable function.

Function Fundamentals, Part 2: Advanced Functionality Techniques

Let's continue our function journey! In this chapter, we'll go deeper into techniques that will help you create more sophisticated and flexible functions within your Jenkins pipelines.

Passing Data into Functions

Let's make our functions more versatile.

Example: Deployment with Configurable Parameters

```
def deploy(environment, configFile) {
    sh "deploy-script --env ${environment} --config ${configFile}"
}

stage('Deploy') {
    deploy('production', 'prod-config.yml')
}
```

Return Values: Getting Results

Functions can return values to be used elsewhere in your pipeline:

```
def getLatestTag() {
  sh(script: "git describe --abbrev=0 --tags",
returnStdout: true)
          .trim() // Remove whitespace
}

stage('Build') {
    def tag = getLatestTag()
    sh "docker build -t my-image:${tag} ."
}
```

Advanced Groovy Within Functions

Remember, inside Scripted Pipeline functions, you have the power of Groovy:

- **Loops:** Process multiple items if needed.
- **Error Handling:** Use `try-catch` blocks.
- **String Manipulation, Collections, etc. :** Leverage Groovy's standard library

Default Parameter Values

Make function usage more convenient:

```
def sendNotification(message, channel = 'general') {
    // Logic to send a notification to the specified channel
    sh "slack-notify --message '${message}' --channel '#${channel}'"
}
```

Controlling Function Visibility

- Functions defined at the top level of your `Jenkinsfile` are accessible from anywhere within the pipeline.

- Define functions *inside* a specific `node` or `stage` block to restrict their scope if needed.

Pro Tip: Error Handling

Always consider how your functions should handle unexpected situations. Options include:

1. **Throwing Exceptions:** Allow the pipeline to fail gracefully.
2. **Return Values:** Signal an error with a specific return value.
3. **Global Error Handling:** Jenkins allows `catchError` blocks for top-level error handling.

Example: Retryable Deployment

```
def deployWithRetries(environment, configFile, maxRetries = 3) {
    def attempts = 0
    def success = false

    while (attempts < maxRetries && !success) {
        try {
            sh "deploy-script --env ${environment} --config ${configFile}"
            success = true
        } catch (e) {
            echo "Deployment failed. Retrying..."
            attempts++
        }
    }
}
```

Best Practices

- **Consider Shared Libraries:** For large projects, Jenkins Shared Libraries provide superior function management (we'll have a dedicated chapter on those!).
- **Test Your Functions!** Devise ways to test your functions in isolation, just like regular code.

Resources

- **Groovy Documentation (Language Features)**
  https://www.groovy-lang.org/documentation.html

Practice

Let's step it up a notch!

1. **Existing Function:** Do you have a function in your pipelines you could enhance with either default parameter values or more sophisticated error handling?
2. **New Function Idea:** Think of a complex task in your pipelines that would be well-suited to be encapsulated in a reusable function with several parameters.

Scoping Variables: Understanding Variable Scope in Jenkins

Let's dive into the sometimes-tricky world of variable scopes in Jenkins. Understanding scope is vital to ensure your pipelines behave predictably and to avoid unintended side effects.

Why Scope Matters

1. **Clarity:** Knowing where a variable is accessible reduces confusion and potential errors in your pipeline logic.
2. **Reusability:** Proper scoping influences how easily functions and pipeline elements can be reused.
3. **Namespace Pollution:** Avoiding accidental overwrites of variables with the same name in different contexts.

Types of Scopes in Jenkins

Let's break down the primary scenarios you'll encounter:

1. **Global Scope:**
   - Variables defined at the top level of your `Jenkinsfile`
   - Visible throughout the *entire* pipeline, across all stages and nodes.
2. **Stage Scope:**
   - Variables defined within a specific `stage` block.
   - Accessible only within that stage and any nested stages or steps.
3. **Node Scope**
   - Variables defined within a `node` block.
   - Their lifetime is limited to the actions executed inside that node.
4. **Step Scope (Limited)**
   - Jenkins provides some steps (like `withEnv`) that let you set variables that exist only for the duration of that single step.

Example: Illustrating Scopes

```
def globalVar = "Hello"

pipeline {
    agent any
    stages {
        stage('One') {
            node('linux') {
                def nodeVar = "Linux Node"
                echo "globalVar: ${globalVar}"
                echo "nodeVar: ${nodeVar}"
            }
        }
        stage('Two') {
            echo "globalVar: ${globalVar}"
            // Trying to access 'nodeVar' here would cause an error!
        }
    }
}
```

Best Practices

- **Favor Narrower Scopes:** Unless a variable truly needs to be used throughout your entire pipeline, restrict its scope to minimize naming collisions.
- **Prefixes for Clarity:** Consider adding prefixes to variable names to hint at their scope (e.g., stage_buildNumber).
- **Environment Variables (env):** For values to persist across stages/nodes, use the global env object carefully.

Pro Tip: The 'env' Variable

The special env variable holds environment variables. Changes made to the 'env' within a pipeline will persist into future stages of the same build!

Tricky Situations

- **Closures:** Groovy closures can 'capture' variables from their surrounding scope. Pay attention to this within functions.
- **Parallel Stages:** Variables in parallel stages are isolated from each other (a good thing!).
- **Jenkins Shared Libraries:** Variables in Shared Libraries have their own scoping rules, which we'll cover in a later chapter.

Example: Setting a Build Description

```
stage('Set Description') {
    node {
        env.BUILD_DESCRIPTION = "Version: ${env.BUILD_NUMBER}"
    }
}
// In subsequent stages, you can access env.BUILD_DESCRIPTION
```

Resources

- **Jenkins Pipeline Documentation: Environment Variables**
  https://www.jenkins.io/doc/book/pipeline/jenkinsfile/#environment-variables

Practice

1. **Examine Your Pipelines:** Do you have variables (especially global ones) that could have a narrower scope?
2. **Hypothetical Issue:** Describe a scenario where a variable's scope in your Jenkins pipelines might lead to a bug or unexpected result.

Bash Brilliance: Executing Multiple Lines in the Bash Shell

Let's unlock the power of multi-line Bash commands within your Jenkins pipelines. This skill will enhance your ability to perform complex tasks and streamline your pipeline logic.

Why Multi-line Bash Matters

1. **Readability:** Break down long commands into logical steps, improving pipeline clarity.
2. **Control Flow:** Use loops, conditionals, and other Bash constructs directly within your pipelines.
3. **Encapsulation:** Package up a sequence of shell commands as a pseudo-function.

Methods for Multi-line Execution

Jenkins pipelines primarily offer two ways to handle multi-line Bash:

1. **Triple Quotes (""") : For Simpler Use Cases**

   ```
   stage('Prepare Environment') {
       steps {
           sh """
               mkdir workspace
               cd workspace
               touch results.txt
           """
       }
   }
   ```

2. **The 'script' Block: For Advanced Needs**

   ```
   stage('Complex Task') {
       steps {
           script {
               def status = sh(script: "ls -l && ifconfig", returnStatus: true)
               if (status != 0) {
                   error("Unable to get network information")
               }
           }
       }
   }
   ```

Key Differences

Feature	Triple Quotes	'script' Block
Simpler Syntax	Yes	No
Return Status Access	No	Yes
Works Across Node/Agent Changes	More finicky	Yes

| Groovy Variable Interpolation | Limited | Full Support |

Triple-Quotes: Tips and Tricks

- **Indentation Matters:** Your scripts within triple quotes will be passed to the shell as-is.
- **Variable Expansion:** Use $variableName for Jenkins variables.
- **Escaping:** If you need literal triple quotes inside of your Bash script, escape them with backslashes (\""").

The Power of the 'script' Block

- **Return Status:** Check the exit code to react to command outcomes.
- **Groovy Integration:** Seamlessly use Groovy variables and logic within your Bash scripts.
- **Cross-Node Persistence:** The script block is ideal when your multi-line logic needs to function correctly even if your pipeline switches nodes or agents midway.

Example: Advanced File Processing

```
stage('Processing') {
    steps {
        script {
            def searchTerm = "critical"
            if (sh(script: "grep -l ${searchTerm} *.log", returnStatus: true) == 0) {
                echo "Search term found!"
            } else {
                echo "Nothing to report"
            }
        }
    }
}
```

Best Practices

- **Start Simple, Iterate:** Begin with triple quotes, refactor to script blocks for complexity.

- **Testing Outside Jenkins:** Develop your multi-line Bash scripts in a regular shell for faster debugging.
- **Consider Functions:** Move complex multi-line Bash into dedicated functions, especially in Shared Libraries.

Resources

- **Bash Scripting Guide** : A great general reference for Bash syntax
  http://tldp.org/LDP/Bash-Beginners-Guide/html/index.html

Practice

1. **Transform It:** Do you have a place in your pipelines with a long, single-line sh command? Rewrite it to use multi-line execution for better organization.
2. **Hypothetical Task:** Describe a scenario in your CI/CD workflow where encapsulating a complex set of shell commands as a multi-line Bash script within Jenkins would be highly beneficial.

Job Inception: Creating Jobs from Jobs

Let's explore how to make Jenkins pipelines dynamically spawn other Jenkins jobs, opening a world of workflow automation possibilities.

Why Does This Matter?

1. **Workflow Orchestration:** Break down complex processes into modular jobs, with parent pipelines orchestrating them.
2. **Parallelism:** Launch multiple jobs simultaneously to speed up your CI/CD processes.
3. **Templatization:** Create generic job templates, then use pipelines to customize and trigger them.
4. **Decoupling:** Promote better organization and reusability of your Jenkins jobs.

Jenkins Mechanisms for Job Creation

There are a few primary ways to achieve this within Jenkins:

- **Parameterized Trigger Plugin:**
    - Great for triggering existing parameterized jobs.
    - The parent pipeline provides parameters to customize the child job's behavior.
    - Option to block and wait for the child job to finish.
- **DSL Scripts (Scripted Pipelines):**
    - Use the Jenkins DSL (Domain Specific Language) to define a new job's structure on the fly.
    - Lots of flexibility, but requires more Groovy code within your pipeline.
- **Pipeline: Multibranch Job Plugin**
    - If you're using Multibranch Pipelines, they have some built-in features for triggering downstream jobs in other branches.

Let's Focus on the Parameterized Trigger Plugin (Common Scenario)

Example: Deployment Pipeline

1. **Build Pipeline:** Compiles code, produces artifacts.
2. **Deployment Pipeline (Parent):**
    - Takes parameters (environment: 'staging' vs. 'production', artifact version, etc.).
    - Uses the 'Parameterized Trigger' step to trigger different child deployment jobs based on parameters.

Key Considerations

- **Passing Information:**
    - Parent Job Parameters -> Child Job Parameters
    - Child Job Results -> Back to Parent (if waiting)
- **Blocking vs. Asynchronous:** Should the parent pipeline wait for the child job to complete? This influences your workflow logic.
- **Error Handling:** What if the child job fails? Robust error handling is essential in multi-job setups.

Example: Parameterized Trigger

```
stage('Trigger Deploy') {
    steps {
```

```
        build job: 'Deploy-To-Staging', parameters: [
            string(name: 'ARTIFACT_VERSION', value: '1.2.3'),
            booleanParam(name: 'ROLLBACK_ENABLED', value: false)
        ], wait: false  // Don't wait for the deployment to finish
    }
}
```

Pro Tip: Visualizing Job Relationships

Some Jenkins plugins help visualize the dependencies between parent and child jobs. Consider the Build Pipeline Plugin for this.

Resources

- **Parameterized Trigger Plugin**
  https://plugins.jenkins.io/parameterized-trigger/
- **Jenkins Job DSL Plugin** https://plugins.jenkins.io/job-dsl/

Practice

Consider your current Jenkins usage:

- **Workflow Breakdown:** Are there processes you could modularize, with some jobs triggering others?
- **Potential for Templating:** Do you have similar jobs that differ only slightly in configuration? They might be good candidates for triggering with parameters.

Brainstorm: Let's Architect a Workflow!

Describe a CI/CD scenario you'd like to implement in Jenkins. Brainstorm how breaking it down into multiple jobs, triggered in a parent pipeline, could improve its structure.

Passing the Torch: Passing Parameters Between Jobs

Let's dive into how to make your Jenkins workflows more dynamic by enabling pipelines to communicate through the power of parameters.

Why Parameter Passing Matters

1. **Information Flow:** Carry build artifacts, test results, configuration data, or any critical information between stages of your process.
2. **Customization:** Control the behavior of downstream jobs without hardcoding values directly in their pipelines.

3. **Context-Awareness:** Jobs can react to outcomes or data generated by those that ran before them.

Mechanisms in Jenkins

There are several ways to accomplish this, each with its nuances:

- **Parameterized Trigger Plugin (Common):**
    - The downstream job must be a parameterized job.
    - Clean interface for passing parameters when triggering.
    - Can optionally receive build results back.
- **Global Groovy Variables:**
    - Set a variable in one pipeline, access it in another (if running on the same agent or within a shared workspace).
    - Use with caution – global scope can have unintended side effects.
- **Artifacts:** Archive files in one job, access them via 'Copy Artifact' step in a subsequent job.
- **External Storage:** More complex scenarios might involve temporary files or a database to share data (less common with pure Jenkins pipelines).

Let's focus on Parameterized Trigger Plugin + Groovy (a versatile combo)

Example: Test Results and Deployment

1. **Test Job:** Runs tests, generates a test report file, and captures pass/fail status in a parameter.
2. **Deployment Job (Parameterized):**
    - Takes a 'DEPLOY_ALLOWED' (boolean) parameter.
    - Triggering pipeline sets it based on test outcome.

Parent Pipeline

```
stage('Test and Decision') {
    def testResult = build job: 'Run-Tests', wait: true
    if (testResult.result != 'SUCCESS') {
        error("Tests failed, deployment halted")
    }
}

stage('Trigger Deployment') {
```

```
    build job: 'Deploy-To-Prod', parameters: [
        booleanParam(name: 'DEPLOY_ALLOWED', value: true)
    ]
}
```

Child Pipeline ('Deploy-To-Prod')

```
pipeline {
    parameters {
        booleanParam(name: 'DEPLOY_ALLOWED', defaultValue: false)
    }
    stages {
        stage('Deploy') {
            when { expression { params.DEPLOY_ALLOWED } }
            //  Deployment steps...
        }
    }
}
```

Key Considerations

- **Data Types:** Text (strings), Booleans, choices from a list, etc. are all supported by parameterized jobs.
- **Upstream/Downstream:** The parent job passes parameters *down* to the child, and can also receive results *back up* if needed.
- **Workspace Sharing:** If jobs need to directly share files, they'll likely need to execute on the same agent/workspace.

Pro-Tip: Parameter Naming

Consistent naming (e.g., "buildVersion") across jobs makes your pipeline logic clearer.

Resources

- **Parameterized Trigger Plugin Documentation**
  https://plugins.jenkins.io/parameterized-trigger/

Practice

- **Parameter Potential:** Do you have Jenkins jobs that run sequentially where the results of one could influence the next?
- **Identifying Data:** What kind of information would be beneficial to pass between these jobs?

Expanding Horizons: Exploring Advanced Jenkins Plugins

Let's embark on an expedition into the rich landscape of Jenkins plugins. We'll discover how these plugins can supercharge your CI/CD workflows.

The Power of Plugins

1. **Extend Core Functionality:** Jenkins, at its heart, provides a robust foundation. Plugins add highly specialized features and integrations.
2. **Tailor to Your Needs:** Avoid building from scratch – there's likely a plugin for that common CI/CD task you need.

3. **Community-Driven Innovation:** Jenkins boasts a vibrant community of developers, meaning an ever-growing pool of solutions.

Finding the Right Plugin

- **Jenkins Plugin Directory:** The primary hub for browsing and searching available plugins https://plugins.jenkins.io/
- **Filter Wisely:** Search by keywords, sort by popularity, and check 'actively maintained' status.
- **Documentation:** Always review a plugin's documentation before installing. Look for examples and instructions.
- **Reputation:** Consider the number of installations, update frequency, and any user reviews available.

Categories of Plugins

Let's highlight a few popular categories to give you a sense of the possibilities:

- **Source Code Management:** Enhancements for Git, Subversion, or more niche SCMs.
- **Build Reporting and Visualization:** Generate custom reports, visualize test trends, integrate with code quality tools.
- **Notifications:** Send build updates to Slack, email, HipChat, or other communication platforms.
- **Security:** Plugins for static code analysis, vulnerability scanning, or credentials management.
- **Cloud Integrations:** Provision resources in AWS, Azure, Google Cloud, or interact with Kubernetes clusters.

Example: Enhancing Your Git Workflow

1. **GitHub Pull Request Builder Plugin:** Automatically triggers Jenkins builds when pull requests are opened or updated.
2. **Git Parameter Plugin:** Add parameters to your job based on Git branches, tags, etc.
3. **Post-build Actions:** Send detailed build status updates directly back to the pull request in GitHub.

Pro-Tip: Plugin Compatibility

- Pay attention to the Jenkins version a plugin supports. Plugins designed for much older versions may not work as expected.
- If unsure, install plugins in a test Jenkins environment first.

Managing Plugins

1. **Jenkins UI:** Navigate to "Manage Jenkins" -> "Manage Plugins". Here you can install, update, and disable plugins.
2. **Updates:** Keep your plugins up-to-date for bug fixes, security patches, and new features.
3. **Judicious Use:** While powerful, too many plugins can impact performance. Choose only what you truly need.

Spotlight on a Few Gems

- **Blue Ocean:** A modern and user-friendly UI for Jenkins.
- **Pipeline Aggregator View:** Get a consolidated dashboard across all your pipeline jobs.
- **Role-Based Access Control:** For fine-grained permission management.
- **Throttle Concurrent Builds Plugin:** Prevent too many builds of the same job from running simultaneously, useful if builds are resource-intensive.

Important Note: These are just a few examples! The plugin ecosystem is vast.

Best Practices

- **Start Small:** Add plugins incrementally, testing as you go.
- **Maintain with Care**: Dedicate time to periodically update and review your plugin selection.
- **Community Insights:** Check plugin reviews or forums to learn about common issues or best practices in usage.

Resources

- **Official Jenkins Plugin List:** https://plugins.jenkins.io/

Let's Go Plugin Hunting!

Describe a specific CI/CD workflow enhancement you wish you had in Jenkins. There's a good chance a plugin can help! Try to search and find promising options.

Section 10:
Wrapping Up and Cleaning House

Saying Goodbye: Deleting Forked Repositories

Let's discuss responsible cleanup practices, focusing on removing forked repositories within your version control systems (like GitHub, GitLab, etc.).

This chapter is vital to maintain a tidy development environment and potentially conserve resources.

Why Forked Repositories May Need Deletion

1. **Outdated Forks:** As the original project evolves, a fork you created long ago might become out of sync and irrelevant.
2. **Abandoned Experiments:** You might have forked a repository to try something, and later decided not to pursue that path.
3. **Completed Contributions:** If you forked a repo, made your changes, and had those changes merged back into the upstream project, your fork may no longer be necessary.
4. **Resource Constraints:** Some version control systems might have storage limits or quotas, especially on free plans.

Important Note: This chapter focuses on deleting your own forks, not deleting the original, upstream repository.

Before You Delete...

- **Local Copies:** Verify if you have essential local copies of the forked repository. Back them up if needed.
- **Open Pull Requests:** If you created any pull requests against the upstream repository, either close them or check if you wish to preserve them elsewhere.
- **Issues and Discussions:** Consider if any valuable discussions within the fork's issues tracker need to be archived.

Deletion Procedure (GitHub Example)

We'll use GitHub as our example but other systems (GitLab, Bitbucket) will have similar mechanisms.

1. **Access Your Fork:** Navigate to the forked repository within GitHub.
2. **Settings:** Click the "Settings" tab of the forked repository.
3. **Danger Zone:** Scroll down to the "Danger Zone" section.
4. **Delete:** Click the "Delete this repository" button.
5. **Confirmation:** You'll be prompted to type the repository name to confirm the action. This is a safeguard against accidental deletion.

Bulk Deletion (If Necessary)

- **Tools:** For mass-deleting many forks, exploring third-party tools or scripts carefully can be helpful. Make sure these tools are reputable.
- **GitHub CLI:** The GitHub command-line interface (CLI) potentially offers scripting options for repository management.

Best Practices

- **Periodic Reviews:** Set aside time occasionally to review your list of forked repositories and ask yourself if they are still serving a purpose.
- **Avoid Proliferation:** Fork judiciously. Fork only when you have a clear intention to modify or contribute to the project.

Pro Tip - Archiving Instead of Deleting

Some version control systems might offer an option to "archive" a repository. This makes it read-only but preserves the history, which can be a less drastic alternative to full deletion, if you're unsure.

Cleaning Up Other Remnants

- **Local Clones:** Delete local folders of the forked code if you don't need them anymore.
- **Webhooks and Integrations:** If you set up specific integrations with the fork, check if they should be removed.

Resources

- **GitHub Help: Deleting a Repository**
  https://docs.github.com/en/github/administering-a-repository/deleting-a-repository

Closing Shop: Stopping Docker Containers

Let's dive into how to gracefully and responsibly stop Docker containers when they've completed their work. This chapter is essential for maintaining a clean development environment and releasing those precious system resources!

Why Stopping Containers Matters

1. **Free Up Resources:** Containers running in the background, even if idle, consume some memory and CPU. Stopping them frees up those resources for other tasks.
2. **Clean State:** Keeping only the actively running containers you need improves your project organization.
3. **Prevent Conflicts:** Old containers could potentially cause port conflicts or unintended interference with newer versions of your services.

Methods for Stopping Containers

Docker provides a few ways to manage container lifecycles:

- `docker stop` **(Graceful Shutdown):**
  - Sends a signal to the main process inside the container, allowing it to potentially perform cleanup tasks (saving data, etc.).
  - The preferred method for most use cases.
  - Example: `docker stop <container-id>` or `<container-name>`
- `docker kill` **(Forceful Termination):**
  - Sends a more abrupt signal to terminate the process.
  - Use if `docker stop` doesn't work (the container is frozen).
- `docker rm` **(Stop and Remove):**
  - Stops the container *and* deletes it entirely.
  - Use when you won't need the container anymore.

Important Considerations

- **Data Persistence:** If your container stores data (a database, for instance), ensure you have a volume or other mechanism to persist data *outside* the container before using `docker rm`.
- **Restart Policies (`:--restart` flag):** Some containers might automatically restart if stopped unless their restart policy is modified.

Stopping Multiple Containers

- **By Label:** If you launched containers with labels, you can filter them for stopping.
  - Example: `docker stop $(docker ps -q -f label=myproject)`

- **docker-compose down:** If using Docker Compose, this command stops containers defined in your compose file.

Example Workflow: Updating a Service

1. `docker-compose pull my-service` # Fetch the latest image
2. `docker-compose up -d my-service` # Recreate, now using the new image
3. `docker stop $(docker ps -q -f label=oldversion)` # Stop the old version (if needed)

Pro-Tip: Automatic Cleanup

Consider the `--rm` flag during `docker run` to have containers automatically delete themselves when stopped. This is great for short-lived tasks.

Best Practices

- **Design for Clean Exits:** Structure your applications inside containers to handle shutdown signals gracefully.
- **Orchestration Tools:** For complex setups, tools like Kubernetes offer more sophisticated container lifecycle management.

Resources

- **Docker Stop Documentation**
  https://docs.docker.com/engine/reference/commandline/stop/
- **Docker Compose Down Documentation**
  https://docs.docker.com/compose/reference/down/

Practice: Container Audit

Let's take a look at your current environment:

1. Use `docker ps` to list your running containers.
2. Identify any containers that could potentially be stopped to free up resources.

Tidying Up: Deleting Unused Volumes

Let's talk about decluttering your Docker environment! Unused volumes can linger, taking up disk space. In this chapter, we'll learn how to identify them, clean them up safely, and put practices in place to manage volumes effectively.

Why Reclaiming Volume Space Matters

1. **Disk Usage:** Especially in development environments, old volumes can accumulate, slowly eating up storage.
2. **Organization:** A proliferation of volumes makes it harder to understand what data is actively being used.
3. **Portability:** When you don't have stale volumes hanging around, it's easier to move your containerized applications.

Understanding Docker Volumes

A quick refresher before we start cleaning:

- **Volumes:** Are designed to store data that needs to persist independently of a container's lifecycle.
- **Named Volumes:** You explicitly create them (`docker volume create mydata`).
- **Anonymous Volumes:** Docker generates them if you don't specify a name. Harder to track.

Identifying Unused Volumes

- `docker volume ls`: Lists all your Docker volumes.
- `docker volume inspect <volume-name>`: Shows details, but importantly, whether the volume is actually attached to any containers.

The Cleanup Process

1. Important: Backups First

- If unsure about a volume's contents, either:
    - Attach it to a temporary container and explore.
    - Create a backup if the data is potentially valuable.

2. Removing Unused Volumes

* **`docker volume prune`:** This is the safest option. It removes *all* unused volumes, prompting for confirmation.

* **`docker volume rm <volume-name>`:** Removes a specific volume by name. Use with caution!

Proactive Volume Management

1. **Use Named Volumes:** Makes managing them easier and avoids anonymous volumes piling up.
2. **Cleanup During Development:** Make it a habit to remove old test containers and their volumes (`docker container prune`)
3. **Lifecycle Policies:** Consider orchestration tools (Kubernetes, Swarm) with more advanced volume cleanup options.

Special Cases: Removing Even Used Volumes

- **Data Migration:** If you need to move data *within* Docker, create a new volume, copy the data over, then delete the old one.
- **Intentional Deletes:** Sometimes you might want to force delete a volume even if it's used. Ensure you understand the implications for your application!

Example: Cleaning Up After Experimentation

1. `docker container ls -a` # List all containers (even stopped)
2. Identify containers from past experiments.
3. `docker container rm <container-ids>` # Delete them
4. `docker volume prune` # Clean up any orphaned volumes

Best Practices

- **Document Volume Purpose:** If it's not obvious from the name, add a description when you create a volume.
- **Monitoring:** For production systems, consider disk monitoring tools to alert you if Docker volumes grow unexpectedly large.

Resources

- **Docker Volume Documentation**
  https://docs.docker.com/storage/volumes/

Practice: Volume Inspection

Let's analyze your Docker environment:

1. Use `docker volume ls` to get a list of your existing volumes.
2. Choose 2-3 volumes and use `docker volume inspect` on them. Can you determine if they're actively in use?

Section 11:
Jenkins Administration

System Configuration Essentials: Configuring Jenkins for Optimal Performance

Let's delve into the art of configuring your Jenkins installation to make it fast, responsive, and tailored to your specific CI/CD workflows.

Why Configuration Matters

1. **Responsiveness:** A poorly configured Jenkins can feel sluggish, impacting your team's productivity.
2. **Scalability:** As your projects and usage grows, the right settings ensure Jenkins can keep up with the demand.
3. **Customization:** Jenkins' flexibility shines when configured to align closely with your team's ways of working.

Key Areas of Focus

We'll go through crucial areas within Jenkins' "Manage Jenkins" -> "Configure System" section:

- **Jenkins Location**
    - Jenkins URL: Make sure this is correct for users and integrations.
    - System Admin e-mail Address: For crucial alerts.
- **Executors**
    - Number of executors: The baseline concurrency for your builds. Too few creates bottlenecks, too many overloads the system.
    - Node configurations: Settings for master node and any agents you connect, impacting available resources for builds.
- **Security**
    - Authorization: Choose between Matrix-based security (fine-grained) or Project-based Matrix Authorization for simpler setups.
    - Enable HTTPS if not already.
- **Tools**
    - Tool Locations: Paths to JDKs, Maven, etc., if Jenkins needs to auto-manage them.
- **SCM Checkout**
    - Timeouts: Prevents builds from hanging indefinitely due to SCM issues.

- **Build Queue**
    - Strategies: For example, prioritize builds by label/branch for critical pipelines.

Performance Considerations

- **Hardware:** Jenkins benefits from a decent amount of RAM and a reasonably modern CPU, especially if you have many concurrent builds.
- **Storage:** If you retain a large number of build artifacts or logs, make sure you have ample disk space. Fast storage (SSD) is ideal.
- **Network:** Jenkins communicating with source control systems (e.g., GitHub) and agents relies on good network connectivity.

Pro-Tips

- **Smaller, Faster Builds:** Strive for modular builds, as they generally fare better with concurrency.
- **Distributed Builds:** Use agents to offload workloads from the Jenkins main server.
- **Version Control Settings:** If possible with your SCM, consider webhooks rather than constant polling for more efficient change detection.

Important: Changes to system configuration often require a Jenkins restart to take effect.

Best Practices

- **Document Your Settings:** Keep notes on why you chose specific configurations, making it easier to reason about them in the future.
- **Version Control Your Config:** Advanced users can use the Configuration as Code plugin for a more maintainable setup.
- **Start Conservatively:** Begin with modest executor counts, increase based on monitoring real-world usage.

Monitoring Jenkins

Pay attention to:

- **Build Queue:** Look for backlogs.
- **System Information (Manage Jenkins)**: CPU usage, memory, etc.
- **Plugins:** Plugins can introduce performance overhead. Monitor the impact of newly added ones.

Example: Tuning for Concurrent Builds

1. **Observe:** How many builds do you typically need to run simultaneously?
2. **Executor Baseline:** Start with that number of executors on your Jenkins master.
3. **Capacity Planning:** If you use agents, factor in their executors as well. Think about how many builds might run in bursts.

Resources

- **Managing System Configuration (Jenkins Documentation)**
  https://www.jenkins.io/doc/book/managing/system-configuration/

Practice: Analyzing Your System

Let's review your current Jenkins installation:

- **Build Habits:** How many concurrent builds are common in your team?
- **Resource Usage:** Do you have any existing monitoring tools for Jenkins?
- **Future Growth:** Do you anticipate your CI/CD workloads to increase significantly in the near future?

Let's Optimize!

Based on your answers, we can pinpoint areas of your Jenkins configuration that might benefit from adjustments.

User Management: Managing User Accounts and Permissions

Let's dive into the realm of Jenkins user management. We'll cover how to create and control user accounts, establish permissions, and ensure your Jenkins environment remains both accessible and secure.

Why User Management is Essential

1. **Security:** Proper access control is a pillar of a secure CI/CD system.
2. **Traceability:** Knowing who initiated builds or changed settings is important for troubleshooting and auditing.
3. **Collaboration:** Different team members might require different levels of access within Jenkins.

Security Strategies in Jenkins

Jenkins offers a few ways to handle user accounts and their permissions:

- **Jenkins' own user database:** Simplest for smaller setups. Users are managed directly within Jenkins.
- **LDAP:** Integrate with an external directory service like Active Directory. Common in larger organizations.
- **Delegate to SCM:** Leverages users and groups from your source code management system (might be limited).

Authorization: What Can Users Do?

Jenkins offers two primary permission systems:

1. **Matrix-based security:** Fine-grained control over various Jenkins actions (build jobs, configure agents, etc.). More flexible.
2. **Project-based Matrix Authorization Strategy:** Simpler setup, ties permissions directly to specific jobs.

Best Practices (Matrix-Based)

- **Groups:** Create groups based on roles within your team (developers, testers, DevOps), making permission management easier.
- **Principle of Least Privilege:** Grant only the minimum permissions necessary for users to do their jobs.
- **Avoid Global 'Admin':** Limit the number of users with full administrative access.

Focus on Project-Based Authorization

- Great starting point for many teams.
- Permissions like Read, Build, Configure tied directly to specific Jenkins jobs.

Creating and Managing Users

1. **Manage Jenkins -> Manage Users**
2. **Create User**
   - Username, password, full name, and email.
3. **Configuring Permissions:**
   - Matrix-based: A table where you check specific permissions.
   - Project-based: Associated with jobs themselves.

Example: Developer Role

- **Overall - Read**
- **Job**
  - Build, Read, Workspace
- **Credentials - View** (If needed)

Pro-Tip: Document Your Permissions

Maintain a plain-text document describing your role/group structure and the associated Jenkins permissions. This aids in onboarding and security reviews.

Security Considerations

- **Strong Passwords:** Enforce password complexity if using Jenkins' own database.
- **API Tokens:** Users can generate these for integrations, treat them like passwords.
- **2FA Plugins:** Consider plugins to add two-factor authentication for enhanced security.

Important: Regularly review users and permissions, especially if team members' responsibilities change.

Resources

- **Jenkins Wiki: Security** https://wiki.jenkins.io/display/JENKINS/Security
- **Matrix Authorization Strategy Plugin Documentation** https://plugins.jenkins.io/matrix-auth/

Practice: Permissions Audit

Let's review your current Jenkins users and their permissions:

1. **User List:** Do you recognize every user? Are there any inactive accounts?
2. **Role Mapping:** Could you define a few common roles within your team that would simplify permission management?

Let's Design a Role!

Describe a typical team member's role (e.g., junior developer). Brainstorm the Jenkins permissions they'd likely need to fulfill their tasks effectively.

Plugin Management: Installing, Updating, and Removing Jenkins Plugins

Let's explore the world of Jenkins plugins, how to install, update, and remove them. Mastering plugin management is vital for customizing your Jenkins environment to perfectly suit your team's workflow.

The Power of Plugins

1. **Extend Core Functionality:** Jenkins plugins are its superpower. They add features far beyond the essentials.
2. **Tailor Your Experience:** Choose plugins that align closely with your team's specific tools and processes.
3. **Vast Ecosystem:** The Jenkins community maintains a huge repository of plugins for a wide variety of use cases.

Managing the Plugin Lifecycle

1. Installation

- **Manage Jenkins** -> **Manage Plugins** -> **Available** tab
- **Search Bar:** Find plugins by name or keywords
- **Checkbox + Install:** Select desired plugins. Be mindful of dependencies (other required plugins).
- **Restart Option:** Choose "Install after restart" for a smoother process, especially for large plugins.

2. Updates

- **Manage Jenkins** → **Manage Plugins** -> **Updates** tab
- **Available Updates:** Jenkins checks for new versions of your installed plugins.
- **Selective or Bulk Updates:** Choose which to update, and when.
- **Restart Consideration:** Some updates may require a Jenkins restart to take effect.

3. Removal

- **Manage Jenkins** -> **Manage Plugins** -> **Installed** tab
- **Checkbox + Uninstall:** Select plugins you no longer need.
- **Caution:** Check if other plugins depend on the one you're removing.

Finding the Right Plugins

- **Official Jenkins Plugin Directory:** https://plugins.jenkins.io/

- Browse by category, popularity, etc.
- **Community Recommendations:** Forums, blogs, and your professional network are great sources of suggestions.

Best Practices

- **Test Thoroughly:** Install or update plugins in a staging environment first, if possible, to catch potential issues.
- **Conservative Updates:** It's sometimes wise to wait a little after a plugin update before installing, to let others discover any unexpected bugs.
- **Documentation:** Always refer to a plugin's documentation for configuration and usage instructions.
- **Avoid Bloat:** Install only what you truly need, as too many plugins can impact performance.

Security Notes

- **Reputable Sources:** Primarily install plugins from the official plugin repository or trusted vendors.
- **Maintenance:** Look for plugins that are actively maintained with regular updates.
- **Permissions:** Some plugins may request sensitive permissions – review these carefully.

Pro-Tip: Plugin Sets

Consider creating "plugin sets" for common roles. Example: a "developer essentials" set could bundle plugins for code quality, reporting, and deployment tools.

Important: Plugin changes often require Jenkins restarts. Plan updates strategically to minimize disruption to your CI/CD workflows.

Resources

- **Jenkins Wiki - Managing Plugins**
  https://www.jenkins.io/doc/book/managing/plugins/

Practice: Examining Your Plugin Landscape

Let's review your currently installed Jenkins plugins:

- **Do you recognize all of them?** If not, some research might be needed.
- **Are any outdated?** Check for available updates.
- **Usage:** Do you actively use all your installed plugins?

Backup and Restore: Safeguarding Your Jenkins Setup

Let's talk disaster preparedness for your Jenkins environment! In this chapter, we'll cover strategies for backing up critical data, restoring it confidently, and ensuring your CI/CD pipelines can weather unexpected storms.

Why Backups are Non-Negotiable

1. **Protect Your Investment:** Jenkins holds your job configurations, build history, customizations – the result of hours of careful configuration.
2. **Hardware Failures Happen:** Disk failures, server crashes, or accidental deletions can strike.
3. **Fast Recovery:** Minimize downtime when disaster occurs by having a way to restore your Jenkins setup quickly.

What to Back Up

- **JENKINS_HOME directory:** Contains most essential Jenkins data:
    - Job configurations (`jobs` folder)
    - Build records (`builds` folder)
    - System configuration (`config.xml`)
    - Plugins
    - User data
- **Credentials:** If not storing them in an external system.
- **Custom Scripts/Tools:** If they are integral to your Jenkins operations.

Backup Strategies

1. **Simple File Copy:** Periodically copy your JENKINS_HOME directory to a secure location. This is rudimentary but a good starting point.
2. **Version Control:** For critical config files within JENKINS_HOME, consider using Git or similar for change tracking and rollback capability.
3. **Plugins:** Specialized plugins exist for Jenkins backups, offering scheduling and more sophisticated options.
4. **Full System Snapshots:** If Jenkins runs in a VM, include it in your VM or cloud snapshot strategy.

Restoration Process

The exact process depends on your backup method, but generally:

1. **Stop Jenkins:** Prevent new data writes while restoring.
2. **Restore Files:** Place backup data back into the correct location, replacing old JENKINS_HOME if needed.
3. **Plugins:** You might need to reinstall plugins if they were not part of your backup.
4. **Start Jenkins:** Verify everything is working as expected.

Backup Destination

- **Separate Server:** Reduces impact if your Jenkins server has a major problem.
- **Cloud Storage:** (AWS S3, etc.) Offers durability and geographic redundancy options for extra protection.

Frequency and Retention

- **Frequency:** Align it with how frequently your Jenkins environment changes. Daily is common, more often for critical, actively changing setups.
- **Retention:** Keep multiple backups over time (e.g., a week's worth of dailies) to restore from different points.

Testing Your Backups

- **Essential:** Never assume backups work until tested.
- **Periodically:** Perform a full restore to a test Jenkins instance. Ideally on separate hardware.

Best Practices

- **Document Your Process:** Have clear instructions for restoration in case the primary Jenkins admin isn't available.
- **Automate:** If using scripts or plugins, schedule backups to run automatically.
- **Security:** Protect your backup files just like you would production data. Encryption might be necessary depending on sensitivity.

Pro Tip - Thin Backups Plugin

This plugin can help manage JENKINS_HOME size by deleting old build records automatically, reducing what needs to be backed up.

Example: A Disaster Recovery Scenario

Imagine your Jenkins server's hard drive fails. Let's outline the steps you would take, assuming you have regular backups:

1. Provision new hardware (or a VM) for Jenkins.
2. Install Jenkins.
3. Stop the fresh Jenkins instance.
4. Restore your latest `JENKINS_HOME` backup onto the new server.
5. Start Jenkins and verify jobs, build history, etc., are present.

Resources

- **Jenkins Wiki - Backup** https://wiki.jenkins.io/display/JENKINS/Administering+Jenkins
- **Thin Backups Plugin** https://plugins.jenkins.io/thinBackup/

Practice: Assessing Your Backup Readiness

Let's discuss your current situation:

- **Do you have a backup strategy for Jenkins?** Describe it.
- **When was your last test restore?** Was it successful?

Monitoring and Logging: Keeping an Eye on Jenkins Performance

Let's discuss how to keep a watchful eye on the health and performance of your Jenkins installation. Think of this chapter like a control panel for your CI/CD infrastructure!

Why Monitoring Matters

1. **Proactive Problem Solving:** Catch issues early, before they cause major build failures or delays.
2. **Bottleneck Identification:** See where your pipelines are slowing down, allowing for optimization.
3. **Capacity Planning:** Track how Jenkins handles load over time, helping you anticipate when to scale resources.
4. **Troubleshooting:** Well-structured logs are crucial when things do go wrong.

Key Areas to Monitor

- **System-Level Metrics**
    - CPU usage of the Jenkins server
    - Memory usage
    - Disk space (especially where builds and artifacts are stored)
    - Network I/O (if relevant to your setup)
- **Jenkins-Specific Metrics**
    - Build queue length: Are many builds waiting?
    - Average build durations: Is anything taking unexpectedly long?
    - Executor availability: Are enough executors online for the workload?
    - Number of builds in progress
- **Log Files**
    - Jenkins' own logs (`jenkins.log`, etc.)
    - Build logs (for individual jobs)

Monitoring Strategies

Let's look at the various ways you can gain insights:

1. **Jenkins UI**

- **Manage Jenkins -> System Information:** Gives a basic snapshot.
- **Load Statistics:** Graph of build trends.
- **Manage Nodes:** Overview of agents and their status.
2. **Plugins**
    - Plugins offer enhanced dashboards, graphs, historical data reporting, etc. Browse the plugin directory!
3. **External Monitoring Tools**
    - **Prometheus:** Popular for metrics collection, works with many Jenkins plugins.
    - **Grafana:** Build visually rich dashboards using Prometheus data or those from other plugins.
    - **Traditional IT Monitoring:** Consider incorporating Jenkins metrics into your existing system monitoring tools if they are flexible enough.

Jenkins Logging

- **Location:** Default logs can be found within your JENKINS_HOME directory.
- **Log Levels:** Adjust verbosity if needed (Manage Jenkins -> System Log) for troubleshooting.
- **Analyzing Logs:**
    - Simple text editor or grep for basic searching.
    - More advanced log analysis tools might be useful for large setups.

Important Note: Log rotation is crucial. Have a policy to prevent logs from consuming all your disk space.

Pro Tip: Set Up Alerts

Configure your tools to send alerts when critical metrics exceed thresholds (e.g., low executor availability, disk space near full) so you can act before problems arise.

Best Practices

- **Start Simple, Expand as Needed:** Don't get overwhelmed. Begin with Jenkins' built-in views and add tools as the complexity of your pipelines grows.

- **Centralize:** If possible, send Jenkins metrics and logs to a central location for better analysis across the board.
- **Correlate with Other Data:** Compare Jenkins metrics to release timelines, code changes, etc., to spot potential patterns.

Resources

- **Monitoring Plugin (Jenkins)** https://plugins.jenkins.io/monitoring/
- **Metrics Plugin (Jenkins)** https://plugins.jenkins.io/metrics/

Practice: Analyzing Your Current Setup

Let's take a look at your Jenkins and identify:

- **Monitoring Tools in Use:** Are you using any plugins or external systems?
- **Metrics:** Which key metrics would be most important for you to track regularly?
- **Pain Points:** Have you experienced any performance issues with Jenkins in the past?

Security Best Practices: Securing Your Jenkins Environment

This chapter is devoted to security, as a poorly secured Jenkins installation can be a prime target for attackers.

Why Jenkins Security is Crucial

1. **Sensitive Data:** Jenkins often has access to API keys, repository credentials, and build environment secrets. A breach is serious.
2. **Attack Vector:** If compromised, Jenkins could be used to infiltrate your development networks further.
3. **CI/CD Disruption:** Attacks can disrupt your pipelines, sabotaging your ability to deliver software.

Key Areas of Focus

- **Access Control** We discussed this in the user management chapter, but it's paramount for security as well.
- **Credentials Management:** Storing secrets safely is non-negotiable.
- **Web Interface Protection:** Jenkins exposed to the internet is particularly vulnerable.
- **Least Privilege Everywhere:** For users, agents, and Jenkins itself.
- **Staying Updated:** Jenkins, its plugins, and the underlying server OS all need security patches.

Authentication and Authorization

- **Strong Passwords:** Enforce complexity rules if using Jenkins' own user database.
- **2FA:** Consider a plugin to add Two-Factor Authentication for an extra layer of protection.
- **SSO Integration:** If your organization uses an Identity Provider (IdP), leverage it with Jenkins for centralized access management.

Safeguarding Secrets

- **Jenkins Credentials Store:** Use it for storing API keys, passwords, etc.
- **Hashicorp Vault (or similar):** For greater scalability and auditing of secret access, consider external secret management systems.

- **Environment Variables:** Use with caution; they might be exposed in logs or build environments.

Network Security

- **Avoid Public Exposure:** If possible, keep Jenkins within a protected internal network.
- **HTTPS:** Absolutely essential. Configure Jenkins with a proper SSL/TLS certificate.
- **Firewalls:** Limit traffic to Jenkins ports only from trusted sources (other build servers, dev machines).

Best Practices

- **Principle of Least Privilege:** Limit users, service accounts, and agents to the minimum permissions they need to function.
- **Security Audits:** Periodically review Jenkins users, plugins, and open ports on the server.
- **Minimize Attack Surface:** Disable unused features of Jenkins; keep your plugin set lean.
- **Monitor Jenkins Logs:** Look for suspicious activity like unexpected logins from odd locations.
- **Disaster Recovery Plan:** Include how to restore Jenkins securely from backups in the event of an incident.

Pro Tip: "Pipeline as Code" Security

If using Jenkinsfiles for pipeline definitions, store them in version control alongside your application code. They can be security audited just like the rest of your project.

Staying Updated

- **Jenkins Core Release Updates:** Check https://www.jenkins.io/ security advisories regularly and patch quickly.
- **Plugin Updates:** Do the same; vulnerable plugins are a common attack vector.
- **Operating System:** Don't neglect to patch the OS Jenkins runs on.

Security Mindset

Technical measures are important, but it's equally crucial to foster a security-conscious attitude throughout your team. Make security part of how your pipelines are designed.

Resources

- **Jenkins Security Documentation**
  https://www.jenkins.io/doc/book/security/
- **OWASP Cheat Sheet - Jenkins Security**
  https://cheatsheetseries.owasp.org/cheatsheets/Jenkins_Security_Cheat_Sheet.html

Practice: Security Review

Let's examine your Jenkins setup with a security focus:

- **Authentication:** How do users log in? Are you happy with its robustness?
- **Plugins:** Do you have any plugins installed that handle sensitive operations? Are they well-maintained?
- **Secrets:** How and where are you storing credentials for external systems?

Let's Brainstorm

Is there one clear area where you could enhance the security of your Jenkins environment?

Section 12:
Jenkins Integration and Extensibility

Integrating Jenkins with Other Tools: Seamless Integration for Enhanced Workflows

Let's explore how Jenkins can play even more nicely with your broader DevOps ecosystem. In this chapter, we'll cover integrating Jenkins with various tools to streamline your workflows and create a connected, automated toolchain.

The Power of Integration

Why limit Jenkins to just build and test? Integrating it with other tools unlocks:

- **End-to-End Automation:** From a code commit to production deployment, Jenkins can orchestrate the whole process.
- **Centralized Visibility:** Jenkins becomes a hub to see the status of tasks happening in other systems.
- **Less Context Switching:** Developers don't need to jump between as many tools.

Common Integration Categories

- **Source Control:** We covered GitHub in depth, but Jenkins works with GitLab, Bitbucket, Subversion, etc.
- **Issue Tracking:** Jira, Bugzilla, etc. Jenkins can update issue states or add comments based on build results.
- **Artifact Repositories:** Artifactory, Nexus… for storing build outputs in a structured way.
- **Deployment Tools:** Ansible, Kubernetes, cloud provider CLIs can be triggered from Jenkins pipelines.
- **Notification Systems:** Slack, email, Microsoft Teams – send build status updates.

- **Monitoring Tools:** Feed Jenkins data into Prometheus or Datadog to correlate build metrics with system health.

Integration Methods

1. **Plugins:** The Jenkins plugin ecosystem is rich. Search for plugins specific to the tools you use.
2. **Jenkins REST API:** Even if there's no plugin, you can use Jenkins' API with HTTP requests within your pipelines to control other tools.
3. **Webhooks:** Many tools can send webhooks (notifications with payload data) to trigger Jenkins builds.

Pro-Tip: Pipeline as Code + Version Control

If storing Jenkinsfiles in version control, you can integrate configuration changes of your integrations themselves into your review process!

Example Integrations

Let's outline a few typical scenarios to illustrate the concepts:

- **Jira Ticket Update:**
    - Pipeline Stage: Post-build
    - Goal: If a build succeeds, transition the associated Jira issue to "Ready for Testing."
    - Method: Likely a Jenkins plugin for Jira
- **Deploy to Staging:**
    - Pipeline Stage: After successful tests, assuming necessary approvals.
    - Goal: Deploy the build artifact to a staging environment.
    - Method: Jenkins executing a Kubernetes deployment script or calling an Ansible playbook.
- **Slack Notification:**
    - Pipeline Stage: Start and End (success or failure)
    - Goal: Keep the team informed without them needing to check Jenkins constantly.
    - Method: Slack plugin for Jenkins

Best Practices

- **Iterative Integration:** Start with one or two critical tools, then expand as you gain experience.

- **Automation as a First-Class Citizen:** Think about integrations while designing your pipelines, not as an afterthought.
- **Centralized Configuration:** If possible, store configuration details (API tokens, URLs for other systems) as Jenkins credentials for easy management.
- **Error Handling:** Make your integrations robust; expect occasional failures from external tools.

Resources

- **Jenkins Plugin Directory:** https://plugins.jenkins.io/
- **Jenkins REST API Docs:** https://www.jenkins.io/doc/book/using/remote-access-api/

Practice: Brainstorming Your Connected Toolchain

Consider your current development workflow:

1. **Existing Tools:** Which tools do you use besides Jenkins (issue tracking, deployment, etc.)?
2. **Pain Points:** Where is a lot of manual work or hand-off happening between these tools?

Extending Jenkins with Custom Plugins: Building and Installing Custom Plugins

Let's venture into the realm of building your own Jenkins plugins! This chapter is for those who want to customize Jenkins further, filling those functionality gaps where off-the-shelf plugins come up short.

Why Build a Custom Plugin?

- **Unique Needs:** If your team has a workflow unlike anyone else's, a custom plugin can streamline it perfectly.
- **Tight Integration:** Maybe you have a proprietary internal tool – a plugin can provide a first-class Jenkins experience for it.
- **Legacy Systems:** Sometimes you need Jenkins to bridge the gap to older, less-standard systems.
- **Learning Experience:** Building plugins is a great way to gain deeper Jenkins knowledge.

Important Note: Before embarking on custom development, make absolutely sure there isn't an existing plugin (or a combination) that gets you close enough.

Prerequisites

- **Java Development:** Jenkins plugins are written in Java. Solid Java understanding is a must.
- **Maven (or similar):** To manage your plugin project and dependencies.
- **Jenkins Development Environment:** A test Jenkins instance to experiment with.

The Structure of a Plugin

At a minimum, a Jenkins plugin needs:

- **Java Classes:** Where your logic lives – actions triggered in the UI, build steps, etc.
- **Jelly Files:** These define small pieces of UI Jenkins uses, if your plugin adds new interface elements.
- **Descriptor:** Metadata telling Jenkins about your plugin.
- **POM File (Maven):** Describes the project, its dependencies, how to build it, etc.

Development Workflow

1. **Jenkins Plugin SDK:** The easiest way to start is using archetype to generate the base project structure
    - Instructions: https://www.jenkins.io/doc/developer/tutorial/create/
2. **Development:**
    - Write Java code for your plugin's functionality.
    - Extend core Jenkins classes and interfaces.
3. **Build the .hpi File:** Maven (or a similar build tool) packages your plugin into a single installable file.
4. **Test in Your Jenkins:**
    - Manage Jenkins -> Manage Plugins -> Advanced Tab -> Upload your .hpi file.
5. **Iterate:** Develop, build, test, repeat!

Example: Custom Notifier

Let's imagine a scenario. Your team has a quirky internal chat tool. Here's how you could build a plugin to send build notifications to it:

- **Logic:** A Java class that handles sending messages to your chat tool (likely using their API or library).
- **Integration Point:** Extend Jenkins' `Notifier` class to tie your plugin into the post-build actions.

Best Practices

- **Start Simple:** Your first plugin doesn't need to be groundbreaking. Get the basics of the workflow down.
- **Version Control:** Use Git or similar for your plugin code.
- **Leverage the Community:** Jenkins development docs and forums are valuable resources for specific problems.
- **Document:** Make a README for your plugin, even if it's internal. You'll thank yourself later.

Advanced Topics

- **Complex UI:** Research more advanced Jelly techniques or explore using JavaScript and React within plugins.
- **Persistence:** If your plugin stores data, consider Jenkins' data management mechanisms.

- **Distribution:** If your plugin is useful to others, learn how to publish it in the Jenkins plugin repository.

Resources

- **Jenkins Plugin Development Docs:** https://www.jenkins.io/doc/developer/
- **Jenkins Plugin Tutorial:** https://www.jenkins.io/doc/developer/tutorial/

Practice: Brainstorming a Plugin Idea

Think about your day-to-day tasks in Jenkins:

- **Repetitive Actions:** Are there several clicks you always perform? A plugin could automate them.
- **Missing Information:** Do you wish Jenkins displayed some data it doesn't natively? Maybe you could fetch it via a plugin.

Integrating Jenkins with Cloud Services: Leveraging Cloud Resources for Scalability

Let's explore how Jenkins and the cloud can form a powerful alliance for scalable, flexible CI/CD. This chapter will cover integrating Jenkins with popular cloud platforms and the benefits they bring.

Why the Cloud and Jenkins Are a Great Match

1. **Elasticity:** Spin up build agents on-demand as your load requires, then scale them back down. Avoid maintaining idle hardware.
2. **Global Reach:** If your team or users are distributed, cloud providers offer regions across the world, potentially speeding up builds closer to the code changes.
3. **Managed Services:** Focus on your pipelines, not on the infrastructure; many cloud platforms provide managed Kubernetes clusters to run Jenkins and agents.
4. **Speed to Setup:** With cloud resources provisioned in minutes, you can experiment and expand quickly.

Key Areas for Integration

- **Jenkins Master:** Running Jenkins itself in a cloud VM gives you control, but also the burden of managing that machine.
- **Build Agents:** Cloud-based agents are the heart of scalable Jenkins in the cloud. We'll cover plugins for the major providers.
- **Infrastructure as Code (IaC):** Define your Jenkins setup (if self-managed), agents, etc., as code for easy replication and recovery (Terraform, CloudFormation, etc.)
- **Artifacts and Storage:** Cloud object storage (like AWS S3) can be ideal for long-term build artifact storage.

Integration with Major Cloud Providers

Let's get a high-level picture of each:

- **AWS**
  - **EC2 Plugin:** Provision traditional EC2 instances as Jenkins agents.

- **Kubernetes Plugin:** Spin up build agents as pods within an Amazon EKS cluster.
- Utilize other AWS services (S3, etc.) alongside your Jenkins pipelines.
- **Azure**
  - **Azure VM Agents Plugin:** Create Azure VMs as agents on the fly.
  - **Kubernetes Plugin:** Leverages Azure Kubernetes Service (AKS) for containerized agents.
  - Deep integration with other Azure DevOps tools, if you use those in your workflow.
- **Google Cloud Platform**
  - **Google Compute Engine Plugin:** Similar concept to EC2 for provisioning VM-based agents.
  - **Kubernetes Plugin:** Integrates seamlessly with Google Kubernetes Engine (GKE).

Pro Tip: Combining Clouds

While focusing on one provider is often simpler, some organizations have multi-cloud setups. Jenkins can work with this, letting you use the best service from each cloud.

Example: Scaling a Build Environment with Kubernetes

Imagine needing to handle sudden spikes in build demand. Here's how a cloud integration could help:

- **Base Setup:** Jenkins master on a small, always-on instance/VM.
- **Agent Config:** A Kubernetes pod definition ready to launch build agents as needed.
- **Jenkins Kubernetes Plugin:** Configured to talk to your cloud's Kubernetes service.
- **Scaling:** Jenkins monitors its build queue; when overloaded, the plugin tells Kubernetes to launch more agent pods.

Best Practices

- **Cost Control:** The cloud is pay-as-you-go. Monitor costs, set budgets, and use auto-scaling wisely to prevent surprises.
- **Security:** Apply the same principles you do to on-premises Jenkins. Credentials need extra care in the cloud.

- **Spot Instances/Preemptible VMs:** Save costs with these non-guaranteed machines for interruptible builds.
- **Hybrid Models:** It's OK to mix permanent Jenkins agents (for some baseline capacity) with cloud-based ones for bursts.

Resources

- **Jenkins Wiki - Cloud Docs:** https://wiki.jenkins.io/display/JENKINS/CloudBees
- **AWS EC2 Plugin:** https://plugins.jenkins.io/ec2/
- **Azure VM Agents Plugin:** https://plugins.jenkins.io/azure-vm-agents/

Practice: Assessing Your Cloud Strategy

Consider your current situation:

- **Scalability Needs:** Do you have predictable build loads, or big spikes?
- **Cloud Usage:** Are you already using a cloud provider? Do you have a mandate to do so?

Jenkins API: Automating Jenkins Tasks with the REST API

Let's unlock the power of programmatic control over Jenkins through its REST API. In this chapter, we'll learn how to manage Jenkins like an application, enabling automation scenarios beyond what's possible from the UI alone.

Why Use the Jenkins API?

- **Advanced Automation:** Chain actions together that would be tedious to perform manually: job creation, node management, etc.
- **External Integration:** Make Jenkins a part of a larger orchestration system controlled by your own scripts or tools.
- **Customization:** If the UI doesn't do exactly what you need, the API might provide a way.
- **Data Fetching:** Pull build metrics, job configurations, and more, for reporting or analysis.

REST API Basics

- **Jenkins Root URL:** Most API URLs start with `https://<your-jenkins>/api/`.
- **API Explorer:** Jenkins has a built-in one: `https://<your-jenkins>/api/`
- **Data Formats:** Jenkins primarily uses JSON for data exchange. Some endpoints can also work with XML.
- **Authentication:** Your Jenkins credentials (username/password or token) are required for most operations.

Common Use Cases

Let's look at some practical examples of what you can do with the Jenkins API:

- **Triggering Builds (with Parameters):** Start a build remotely, even passing in values to its parameters.
- **Creating New Jobs:** Define job configurations as code (XML or JSON), and create them via the API.
- **Node Management:** Add, remove, or view the status of build agents programmatically.

- **Retrieving Build Information:** Get the status of a past build, its console output, or changes since the previous build.
- **Querying the Plugin List:** Handy for generating a report of installed plugins and their versions.

API Interaction Methods

1. **Direct HTTP Requests:** Use tools like `curl` or libraries like Python's `requests` to make calls.
2. **Jenkins CLI:** Provides a command-line interface for many API actions.
   - Docs: https://www.jenkins.io/doc/book/managing/cli/
3. **Client Libraries:** Several languages have libraries that abstract the API into more friendly objects.
   - Example: JenkinsAPI for Python
     https://python-jenkins.readthedocs.io/en/latest/

Example: Creating a Job with Python (`requests`)

Here's a simplified illustration:

```python
import requests
from requests.auth import HTTPBasicAuth

jenkins_url = 'https://your-jenkins-server/'
username = 'your-username'
api_token = 'your-api-token'  # Get this from your Jenkins user profile

job_name = 'my-new-job'
job_config_xml = '''
  <project>
    ... your job XML ...
  </project>
'''

create_job_url = jenkins_url + 'createItem?name=' + job_name
headers = {'Content-Type': 'text/xml'}

response = requests.post(create_job_url, data=job_config_xml, auth=HTTPBasicAuth(username, api_token), headers=headers)
```

```
if response.status_code == 200:
    print('Job created successfully!')
else:
    print('Error:', response.text)
```

Important! Use API tokens for scripts and integrations, rather than your plain-text password, for better security.

Best Practices

- **Understand Rate Limits:** Some Jenkins installations may limit how frequently you can call the API.
- **Error Handling:** Implement robust error handling in your scripts, as network or Jenkins issues can happen.
- **Versioning:** Depending on your Jenkins version, some API details might differ. Refer to docs.

Resources

- **Jenkins REST API Documentation:**
  https://www.jenkins.io/doc/book/using/remote-access-api/

Practice: API Exploration

Use the Jenkins API Explorer (or `curl`) to:

- **List the jobs on your Jenkins.**
- **Get the last 5 build results for a specific job.**

Let's Design an Automation

Describe a repetitive Jenkins management task you currently do manually. Try to outline how you could automate at least part of it using the Jenkins API.

Event-Driven Automation: Triggering Jenkins Builds with Webhooks

Let's explore how to make Jenkins react to events in your wider development ecosystem using the power of webhooks. This chapter is about making your CI/CD pipelines even more responsive and integrated.

What are Webhooks?

- A mechanism for one system to notify another when an event occurs.
- Like a "push" vs. the "pulling" of polling.
- Works via an HTTP request (usually a POST), containing data about the event.

Why Webhooks + Jenkins are Powerful

- **Real-Time Builds:** Trigger builds instantly in response to code pushes, issues created, deployments on other systems, etc.
- **Tighter Integration:** Link events far outside Jenkins into your pipelines, chaining automation together.
- **Less Wasted Resources:** No more polling at intervals when you don't need to, conserving build resources.

How Webhooks Work with Jenkins

There are a few main methods:

1. **Generic Webhook Trigger Plugin:**
   - Provides a configurable Jenkins endpoint.
   - You map event details from the webhook payload to build parameters, if needed.
2. **Specialized Plugins:** Many plugins for GitHub, GitLab, etc., directly understand the webhooks those systems send.
3. **Middleware:** A small service of your own sits between the external system and Jenkins, translating webhooks if needed

Security Considerations

- **Validate the Source:** If possible, check the IP address of incoming webhooks to ensure they originate from expected systems.
- **Secrets:** Avoid sending sensitive data in webhook payloads if you can. Have Jenkins fetch it securely.

- **Endpoint Protection:** If your Jenkins is public, lock down webhook URLs to authorized parties using authentication or firewalls.

Common Use Cases

- **Code Changes:** GitHub, Bitbucket, and similar, can send a webhook on pushes or pull requests. Instant build!
- **Issue Trackers (Jira, etc):** Trigger builds or deployments potentially based on issue state changes.
- **Container Registries:** A new image is pushed? Start a deployment pipeline in Jenkins.
- **Monitoring Systems:** Trigger remediation pipelines in Jenkins based on alerts.

Example: GitHub Pull Request Build Trigger

1. **Install Plugin:** Jenkins has a specific "GitHub Pull Request Builder" plugin that handles GitHub's webhook format.
2. **GitHub Setup:** In your repository, configure a webhook pointing to your Jenkins server, with content type `application/json`.
3. **Jenkins Job Config:**
   - Enable the trigger from the GitHub plugin.
   - Use the provided build parameters to access things like the branch name or pull request number.

Beyond Basic Webhooks

- **Filtering:** Get fancy with plugins like Generic Webhook Trigger: https://plugins.jenkins.io/generic-webhook-trigger/ to trigger only on specific conditions in the webhook data.
- **Response:** Some systems expect an HTTP response back from a webhook. You could even use Jenkins to call another API as a result of the webhook.

Best Practices

- **Start Simple, Expand as Needed:** Basic code-change triggering is a great first use case.
- **Meaningful Payload:** The system sending the webhook should include enough data for Jenkins to make decisions or parameterize the build.
- **Error Handling:** What if the webhook fails or Jenkins is down? Build in retries or logging.

Resources

- **Jenkins Wiki - Webhooks:**
  https://wiki.jenkins.io/display/JENKINS/GitHub+Plugin#GitHubPlugin-GitHubWebhooksandSECURITY
- **Generic Webhook Trigger Plugin:**
  https://plugins.jenkins.io/generic-webhook-trigger/

Practice: Brainstorming Webhook Triggers

Think about your workflow and identify 2-3 events in your tools (issue tracker, version control, etc.) that would be useful to automatically trigger a Jenkins action.

Exploring Jenkins Ecosystem: Discovering Additional Resources and Communities

In this final chapter, we'll venture outside the boundaries of Jenkins itself and explore the vast ecosystem of resources and communities that have grown around this powerful tool. Think of this as your roadmap to continuous learning and support!

Why the Jenkins Ecosystem Matters

- **Knowledge Sharing:** Others have likely faced similar challenges as you; their solutions can save you time.
- **Avoiding Reinventing the Wheel:** The Jenkins community provides a wealth of ready-made solutions and best practices.
- **Finding Support:** When things do go wrong, having a place to ask questions is invaluable.
- **Inspiration:** Seeing how others use Jenkins in innovative ways can spark your own ideas.

Key Areas of the Ecosystem

Let's navigate through the major places you'll want to know about.

1. **Official Jenkins Documentation:**
   - **User Guide:** The core reference for how to use Jenkins' features. https://www.jenkins.io/doc/
   - **Plugin Documentation:** Each plugin should have its own documentation page on the Jenkins site.
   - **Developer Docs:** If you delve into plugin building. https://www.jenkins.io/doc/developer/
2. **Jenkins Blog:** News, feature announcements, and case studies. https://www.jenkins.io/blog/
3. **Online Communities**
   - **Official Mailing Lists:** A classic way to ask questions and participate in discussions.

- **Community Forums:** A more modern, threaded discussion environment. https://community.jenkins.io/
    - **Stack Overflow:** Use the `jenkins` tag. Many general CI/CD questions are also relevant.
    - **Subreddits:** Such as r/jenkinsci
4. **Jenkins Events**
    - **Jenkins World / DevOps World:** The major annual conference, in-person and online portions.
    - **Local Meetups:** Check if there are Jenkins user groups in your area.
5. **The Jenkins Plugin Repository:**
    - The heart of Jenkins' extensibility. Browse, search, and find plugins to solve almost any problem. https://plugins.jenkins.io/

Best Practices for Community Engagement

- **Search First, Ask Later:** Chances are, someone has already had a similar problem to yours. A good search strategy saves everyone time.
- **Be Specific:** Provide clear details about your Jenkins version, relevant plugins, and what you've already tried when seeking help.
- **Contribute Back:** If you solve a tricky problem, share the solution on a forum. Even writing up how you use Jenkins in a blog post is valuable to others.

Pro-Tip: Keep an Eye on the "Roadmap"

The Jenkins project has a public roadmap outlining its future direction. This can give you clues about what new features might be coming natively, so you don't have to rely on plugins long-term.
https://www.jenkins.io/project/roadmap/

Example: Finding Help for an Obscure Issue

Let's imagine this scenario: You have a specific Jenkins build step failing intermittently, and only on certain agents. Here's the approach:

1. **Error Message Decoding:** Google the exact error, including relevant Jenkins version and plugin names.
2. **Plugin Issue Tracker:** Major plugins often use GitHub or similar. Search for open or closed issues that sound like your problem.
3. **Jenkins Issue Tracker:** If it seems like a core Jenkins bug, check https://issues.jenkins.io/

4. **Targeted Forum Post:** If nothing turns up, craft a concise forum post with all the important details.

Staying Up To Date

The Jenkins world moves fast! Here's how to avoid falling behind:

- **Plugin Updates:** Jenkins should notify you of these.
- **Jenkins Core Releases:** Subscribe to the Jenkins blog or announcements mailing list.
- **Community Buzz:** Following Jenkins contributors on social media can give you early heads-up on exciting developments.

Conclusion

Congratulations! You've reached the end of our journey from Jenkins novice to a seasoned pro. Let's reflect on what you've accomplished and look toward the exciting possibilities that Jenkins opens up in your DevOps career.

Recap: Your Jenkins Transformation

- **The Foundations:** You now understand the core principles of CI/CD and how Jenkins embodies them. Setting up Jenkins and building your first pipelines felt like magic made concrete.
- **Gaining Control:** SCM integration, parameters, variables, the Jenkins DSL... all are tools to precisely orchestrate your software delivery process.
- **Mastery:** With advanced techniques like conditional logic, functions, and secrets management, your pipelines became robust and adaptable.
- **Ecosystem Power:** You tapped into the vast plugin library, integrated Jenkins with your other tools, and learned to leverage the wider community.

Continuous Learning is Key

The DevOps landscape, and Jenkins along with it, continue to evolve. Here's how to stay ahead of the curve:

- **Practice and Experiment:** The best way to cement knowledge is to build things. Try out those advanced plugins, or create a mini-project to test an integration idea.
- **Community Connection:** Keep an eye on forums and blogs. Share your own successes and challenges to contribute to the collective knowledge.
- **Revisit the Fundamentals:** Technologies change, but the core concepts of CI/CD and the problems Jenkins solves remain relevant.

The Future is Automated

As you continue to expand your Jenkins expertise, you become an agent of positive change within your teams and organizations. You can:

- **Evangelism:** Help onboard new team members to Jenkins and modern CI/CD practices, spreading efficiency.
- **Problem Solving:** Tackle complex automation challenges, removing bottlenecks, and freeing your colleagues to focus on what they do best – create great software.

- **Mentorship:** More junior DevOps engineers will look to you for guidance. Be generous with your knowledge and take the opportunity to learn yourself when teaching others.

Jenkins: Your DevOps Backbone

Jenkins, while sometimes having a reputation for complexity, offers unmatched flexibility and a thriving ecosystem. The skills you've gained in this book translate far beyond the specifics of any one tool. You've leveled up your ability to design, implement, and champion the processes that will push the boundaries of what your teams can deliver, quickly, reliably, and at scale.

Farewell

I hope this book has been a valuable companion. Now go forth, automate, streamline, and elevate your DevOps career to new heights!

_____
_____
_____

Printed in Great Britain
by Amazon